D1253067

Walking to
Extremes

Howard
McCord

McPherson & Company
KINGSTON, NEW YORK

FARNS
G
465
.M3962
2008

Copyright © 2008 by Howard McCord.
All rights reserved.

Published by McPherson & Company,
Post Box 1126 Kingston, New York 12402,
with assistance from the Literature Program of the
New York State Council on the Arts, a state agency.
Designed by Bruce R. McPherson.
Typeset in Garamond.
Printed on pH neutral paper.
Manufactured in the United States of America.

1 3 5 7 9 10 8 6 4 2   2008 2009 2010

LIBRARY OF CONGRESS CATALOGING-IN-PUBLICATION DATA

McCord, Howard, 1932-
Walking to extremes / by Howard McCord.
    p. cm.
ISBN 978-0-9792018-6-8 (pbk.: alk. paper)
1. McCord, Howard, 1932—Travel. 2. Walking—Anecdotes.
3. Deserts—History—Anecdotes. I. Title.
G465.M3962 2008
910.4092—dc22

                                2008012217

ACKNOWLEDGMENTS

Frontispiece drawing: "Howard on the Jornada" © 2008 by Leila Rotschy McLachlan.
(Detail.) Graphite on paper. Reproduced courtesy of the artist.
Photographs of Iceland on front cover, page 14, and pages 32-33, courtesy
of the photographer, Maxime Homand, copyright © 2005.
Photographs on pages 70, 80, and 134 are by Howard McCord.
"The Apache Kid" first appeared in Exquisite Corpse #51, 1995.
"The Arctic Desert" was first issued in a small edition by Stooge Editions in 1975.
"On Top Again" was published originally in Nova (U. Texas–El Paso), Dec. 1984.
Quotations from the Landnamabok ("Book of Settlements") translated by Hermann
Palsson and Paul Edwards, 1972, are quoted courtesy of University of Manitoba Press.

565185
Lamont Library
Harvard University

OCT 3 1 2008

To Jennifer, always.

AND MY COMPANIONS
IN THE DESERTS OVER THE YEARS
Dan Vickers
David Burwell
Charles Mangus
Richard Ingraham
Brian Richards
John Haynes
Dan, Liela, AND *Peter McLachlan*

Contents

Preface

I GREW UP in the far western tip of Texas, in El Paso, with mountain ranges always in view—the Franklins, the Huecos, the southern end of the Organs, and across the Rio Grande, the Sierra de los Burros, or the Juarez mountains.

The wonderful miles of space between the mountains was the Chihuahuan desert. The invitation to explore was everywhere. I accepted, and if the extent of my wanderings during the past sixty-five years has reached to distant parts of the world, the most vivid memories remain those of the Southwest.

On my earliest venture into the mountains, I remember holding onto my grandmother's hand as she led me up a rocky, cactus-studded mountainside until we were well above our picnic spot. I looked down, then out, then up and up. This was a new world, and I wanted to keep going. A few years later Dan Vickers and I began our explorations of the Franklin mountains that jut into El Paso, and it was not long before we were scrambling over the rocks at Hueco Tanks, hiking up Fillmore canyon in the Organs, and McKittrick and Slaughter canyons in the Guadalupes. David Burwell was an early companion also. We bagged minor peaks and ridges, some so lonely and distant we imagined no one else had ever been so foolish as to make such effort.

Each summer I spent a few weeks at my great-uncles' ranches in New Mexico bordering the Mescalero Apache Reservation and rode patient horses more miles than I then had ever walked, learning something of the cowboy's art. My mother's family had been ranchers in Texas since the days of the Republic, and in

New Mexico since the 1860s. My cousin, Tom Joy, and I hunted jackrabbits each evening, and on the ranch I honed my shooting skills. Aside from wandering on foot, shooting has been my greatest outdoor pleasure, and I am marking my seventieth year as a rifleman as I write.

Then the Korean War came, I joined the Navy after one semester of college, and it was five years before I returned. I found the intellectual life of the academy nearly as fascinating as the mountains and ended spending forty-three years as a professor. I trained as a medievalist and an old-fashioned comparative philologist. The Navy had introduced me to Asia, and my reading deepened my interest. In graduate school I took a course in Indo-European grammar and in Sanskrit and continued wrestling with the language for several years. In 1964 I was invited to teach an Honors course in Eastern Civilizations, and received a Fulbright award to spend three months in India and southeast Asia. This was my first trip abroad not under military constraints, and I enjoyed it very much. I stopped for a week in Greece, and another week in London. A few years later another academic grant enabled me to go to Iceland and Lapland to wander freely and write what I wanted. Later, for four consecutive summers, I went to Alaska for brief teaching sessions and as much brushbusting as I could get in.

But my landscape roots were always Southwestern. I even got a grant "to travel the back roads of the west" and loved doing it. Each summer, grant or not, I found an area I had not been, and went. I keep doing it each summer now with my grown children, and have managed to get the six to come along to some pretty outlandish places. I even attempted a fiftieth anniversary climb of the Wedge in 2000, but what I discovered later was a faltering aortic valve stopped me about halfway up. Two of our party made it, so I count it a qualified success. I had the valve replaced in 2007, and will hope it carries me many miles more.

I had begun to publish poetry in 1953, when I was still in the

Navy, largely through the encouragement of Lafayette Young, who owned The Book Centre in San Diego in the early fifties. He introduced me to contemporary literature and showed me the first "little magazines" I ever encountered. I sent some poems to *Miscellaneous Man* in Berkeley and they were accepted. The issue was confiscated in the famous police raid on City Lights Bookstore which also seized Allen Ginsberg's *Howl* and other offenses to the body politic. I suppose this makes me a real Beat.

These were also good years for short story writers, and in the next decade I had several stories published in which—to me, anyway—the theme of the solitary in a mental wilderness emerged as a fascination. *The Man Who Walked to The Moon* (McPherson & Co., 1997) was the culmination of this theme in fiction, and the present book a further exploration of it in my own life, in the wilderness of landscape. I have never felt a great distinction between poetry and prose. Poetry is composed of "piths and gists" as Pound's student wrote, and prose fills in more gaps. They are both the aesthetic and imaginative uses of language which, as Suzanne Langer said, long before computers, create virtual worlds.

I think my attraction to Iceland and Lapland was that they were nearly unimaginable landscapes until I experienced them. To be alone in the center of Iceland is to be profoundly, wonderfully alone in a desert with ice. The southwestern deserts were more familiar from childhood on, but they too provided that absence of the other, that insulation from the many that was of such interest to me. Even here in the Black Swamp of Ohio I find that I go weeks without speaking with anyone except my wife and Bill Fox, my workout partner at the gym. He and I meet three times a week for an hour. It seems that even in the freedom of retirement, I do not seek society. I presume this is an aberration, but am not moved to correct it.

This wandering has been as important to me for its intellectual worth as all the thousands of books I have read and loved over the years, and given me the core I write from. Landscapes are as informative as words. Perhaps more. There is this physical world that fascinates me, which is the realm of science, my family which I love, and the realm of language and imagination. The rest I am less passionate about, though there is no end of curiosities to examine.

My deepest thanks to Liela McLachlan for her fine artwork, and to the poets Christof Scheele and Mitch Ramsey for magically transforming a messy typescript from a manual Royal into computer-friendly patterns of positives and negatives. To my companions over the years, and to my patient and loving wife, Jennifer, and to my brilliant, wild children—Colman, Robert, Susannah, Julia, Eva, and Wyatt Asher—always ready to go walkabout with dad to discover what's over the ridge.

HOWARD McCORD
January 22, 2008

Walking to
Extremes

The Arctic Desert

I

There is absurdity here and there is darkness,
but they belong to our conceptual systems and
not to existence or the soul.—S. M. ENGEL

*I make these notes hurriedly, copying some from three notebooks
I carried while traveling, and from what memory has left me.*

LIGHT is the dominant element: midnight is gold,
creamy. Noon is silver. I forgot about the stars, and
was astonished by the moon when I saw it again, two
months later. Light does away with stars, which once
seemed such treasures. I never noticed the sun—it
wandered ceaselessly, quietly. Perhaps what I felt is
linked to a phrase I found in myself watching the miles
of the Springisandur before me: *a space on which a kind
of eternity rests.* Stars define time, but light removes it.
Erases it even from the body. Slips it off, and you walk
without a second's shadow darkening your eyes.

·

So much earth and sky are accessible to vision in the interior. My eyes were filled, welling with immensities and brilliance. I was glad for the simplicity of the landscape, for to perceive a city or a forest with that clarity would be an annihilation, senses drowned. It was curious to observe my eyes. Where are things located? What is out there? Music not in the score, a poem not in the words? What is in the landscape? What is in my body? All the minima are observed, a gathering of distances.

.

But there was no awe. Curiously no awe.

.

What we see is how we look. Even asleep, I could feel the light pressing through the tent, pressing my body. Before I came to this place I defined a desert as "an excess of simplicity." Now I am sure of neither of the key words. I would take the word "virtue" in its old alchemical, medical use. Then the desert shifts. A note: "Solitude as its opposite, is both positive and negative, healthful and destructive. Then, is it the *field*, the context (in all ramifications) and the *motion* of the constituents of the *field* which generate the Virtue?"

.

What is the Virtue of *desert*, and what are the correspondences to be maintained? From the *Landnámábok*: "the farm stood where the mountain is now." Mountains ignore time in Iceland, too. They grow like the sky changes. I come to my own rhythms, and must stick by them. I walk at such a pace, no other. Simplicity allows discovery. There is a linkage in the paradigms of clarity, isolation, and freedom.

.

I sit by a second-story window overlooking Main Street. The traffic is relentless in the dark. A few weeks ago I was back at center, looking out toward Arnarfell from a ridge above the Jökuldalur—31 kilometers by line of sight. It looked like two hours' walk. From a week before on a northern cape, at Breithavik, I had seen Grimsey, squatting on the Arctic Circle, its cliff distinct at 52 kilometers. The white walls of the house across the street flicker like moths' wings in the passing headlights. I am enclosed.

.

"A space on which a kind of eternity has focused, and lingered." And the processes of the body, are they caught, too? What do we do when we do nothing? Master Blake tells us "Time is the mercy of Eternity," and so it is. Perhaps I should not even ask, and accept the mercy of so much space. Here on this stairway landing I have surrounded myself with sacred objects. Some have power on their own account, others possess it as an adjunct to friendship, or to a simple wish. A kachina, a magical egg, knives, a feather *pajo* I made of a summer's feathers—feathers the god wind brought to my feet. Baby Krishna with his butter pat, the great mother of the Cyclades, a Tibetan charm, one-half a stone map, a wooden plaque telling me "Haz todo con amor" (and I will, Paul, as I can). Dozens more in the desk drawers, each with a complete story. A thorough accounting would produce an autobiography, for at each turn I have taken I have picked up the physical marker, the marker given. I burned twenty years of letters last May: everything in them is contained in six objects. I took no charm to Iceland, wore no rings to fill with greater light. I brought back a small piece of new lava from Askja, needle-sharp, drawn out and shaped by a dynamics I do not understand.

.

This night I feel these objects wail and grind a singular "I" at me, as though they were parts of my body, as they probably are. But *that* I was freed from in Iceland. I spoke little, I wrote little, I needed no books, no objects such as these to consolidate experience, to stand as substantial symbol and code, my history compressed into matter. Silence and light were sufficient. To celebrate them is to become invisible, even to oneself. I was a deer once, in New Mexico, through Tío Híkuri. In Iceland I had not even a shadow's weight, doing nothing, the distances swallowed in light, and emptiness filling my eyes with a sensation so pure it required no perceiver to exist. White noise, totally, white mind.

I love the genial stupor of long walking. the slow dissolve into footsteps, into one's boots. All that exist are balance, footing, and if the land moves up, thrust. My eyes are 163 centimeters from my toes—I look with my feet, walk with my eyes. In the lava fields a Golden Plower will flutter to a stone, call you away from his mate, follow you a mile, talking, deceiving you.

.

On the fifth day walking, a bird screamed high in the air, from the heights of Singitjakka, an eagle, the first I've ever heard. The cliffs rise a thousand meters there. He was a black speck, circling at the rim. I watched a bit, then put my mind back in plod-time, measuring the rhythms of Nothing.

.

In the black desert, tiny markers of pink, *Armeria*, called *Thrift*, mixed with Moss Campion, the Dwarf Catchfly, *Silena acaulis*. I cannot imagine what creature pollinates them. There must be a species of insane Icelandic bees—tiny, fearless, with a bizarre metabolism. (But it is the wind.) Gnats and midges at Herthubreitharlindir, and wonderful black orb-weavers in the lava, feasting on the gnats. At one camp spot in the lowlands, I found mosquitos dormant, sleeping quietly in the petals of Roseroot, *Sedum rosea*, too cold to fly. That was at Thórsmörk, in the south.

.

The notes continue, beginning with one word in Icelandic: OBYGGDIR, *interior*. In the sagas, VESTRI OBYGD was the western wilderness, perhaps Baffin Island. The Norse Greenlanders called the harsh east coast of Greenland UBYGDER, the "unbuilt" places. No homesteads were found east of Cape Farewell, and the tales run to shipwreck, and desperation. Torgils Orrabeinfostre spent four years making his way to the western settlements after a wreck in 1001. A hard journey, perhaps not even true. But hard.

.

Suddenly I am transfixed with memories of New York City. Walk the street, and flashes of recognition. I think I see acquaintances, hear my name spoken, the shuttling crowd like a loom at work. The physical feeling is a déjà-vu fatigue. Then the weight of the crowds presses down. I look at *American Poetry Review*, and it is an incessant scream to run, run, run, write faster. These people write. They must do it every day, as a sickness, an expiation, a sacrifice demanded by loud noises, movements.

.

I come to my own rhythms, and must stick by them. There is a madness in this City that even Fraenkel did not grasp. I go see *Heavy Traffic*. *It is perfect*. Inside and outside the theater are finally *one*. The topological problem of turning the inner tube inside out is experienced, *is*. The crowd is anxious, bored. Two in the theater sitting next to me drink from a pint flask, and then make acute philosophical observations about the film. Carefully, I look at them. Two young men I would take to be stock clerks, G.I.s, construction workers. One explains to the other the sociological significance of the work observed. When I leave I step over the seat and go behind them. I have no wish to get into a fight.

.

At the Algonquin, George behind the bar tells me that the Japanese are everywhere, with cameras, as before the world war. I should buy Ashland Oil, because *something* is brewing. It is the Chinese who are using the Japanese, as the Germans used the Japanese before WW II. The Chinese will soon have us. He has a son who gets into trouble and then out of it. Wrecks cars regularly, drinks too much. I like George very much. In Narvik, the French boys I roomed with in the hostel told me when I came back from a climb—"The children here, they are all drunk!" They were indignant in their surprise. I would be drunk most of the time if I lived in Narvik too. But not in Iceland. The kids had nothing to do but roar down Kongens Gate on their Kawasakis, drink beer at $1.40 a glass, and rut with local girls, who were at least as bored, and maybe more, with no Kawasakis. I left Narvik the next morning and began my Lapland walk without equipment I might have purchased there. No regrets. George has an excellent memory. We went over a minor occurence two years previously. He remembers. The man involved has now been put away, somewhere in the Carolinas. It has to do with a birthday cake and the CIA.

.   .

I realize the strange independence required, the resolute cantankerousness I must employ. I never felt this in Iceland. "Argue from Phenomena, and do not feign hypotheses," says Newton. OK. OK. In the city, the "something wrong" has a tangibility it lacked before. My fingers do not curl on a glass in quite the same way. I can no longer be abstract. At 11 PM I am in my room, and hear police whistles. Many, many. I expect to hear gunfire. I do not. The next morning I realize that it was the doorman calling cabs. All night I think about Nothing. I play Wittgenstein: "What do we *do* when we do nothing?" What is the difference between the minima of the Desert, and Nothing? Is minima divisible? Can one say, "of line AB, there is first A, then B"? God has no memory, only perception.

.

At home I read Guy Davenport on Agassiz, "The Western world has had three students of metamorphosis. Ovid. Darwin, Picasso." I am assuming he wrote this before Portmann. But it fits the City. In the desert, one does not make up scenarios for the stones; contrariwise, in a New York bar, it is nearly impossible not to. Everyman the dramatist of his proper moments. Across the small room, six people argue *analytically*. It is worse than high school and the heady discovery of logic. At the bar, people dance slowly, standing still. But their talk is movement. Control invites tension. One gentleman's words lick the nipples of the woman beside him, who is talking to another gentleman. There is a contest everyone in the room is playing — Who Is the Best Fuck of All? Alone, in an odd corner, I am a player too. All must play. No coercion. Simple presence is membership. The freer people get, the more they drink, the tighter grows the game. I drink to keep up with the game. I have spoken to no one. George is busy at the bar. He does not need to talk about conspiracies when he can be a part of one. The lady in the alcove is the daughter of a famous radio and film writer, recently retired. She is small, red haired, and boasts only a little. I have no desire to meet anyone present. I remember a line from the *Landnámabok* again: "They left Telemark because of some killings."

.

You see, the desert presents a *task*. New York City presents a burden. I hear a sentence from the bar: "He is careful about his company." So it is here that I should enter Boswell's sentence from his *Corsica*: "Where they make a desart, they call it peace." He found the line in Tacitus.

.

The peace I find resides in imagination, in the gentle whirling of my mind to the rhythm of walking, the loose play of words jostled against one another, jostled enough to make a sweet confusion.... It is the very premise of a notebook.

.

There are two geographic fantasies: the "Antarctic Convergence," and the "Pole of Relative Inaccessibility." I love the latter better.

.

Take, in your mind, a likeness of this earth. Detach the southern hemisphere from the northern. Make a montage of S and N. Notice where Antarctica extends. The northern tip of Iceland is just about where the south magnetic pole is: 66°33′ North or South. A curious number. It measures a 24-hour day, the extremes of. Ask someone for a definition of the Arctic or Antarctic Circles.

.

The wind circles the earth from the west, in the south. That's Coriolis: Do you know which way the Arctic Ocean rotates?

.

In Iceland, the sky is not an acquaintance, I hold no token of friendship. I would not forget something which so surely could not be given.

.

Now, the "Pole of Relative Inaccessibility." 84° North, 160° West. It is the most difficult region to reach by surface travel. A refinement of the old "Ice Pole," marking the center of the polar ice cap (that was held to be 86° N, 157° W), it was nearly attained by Wally Herbert and his friends as they made their way by dogsledge from Point Barrow to Spitsbergen in 1968. I have never been there, am not even interested in going. I would love to walk Kamchatka, or winter in the Jarbidge. I will tell you one day's travel, to Hveravellir.

.

The 48-hour tourist in Iceland often takes a little trip

out to Thingvillir, where the Althing was founded in 930 AD. Then they sometimes go farther, east through green Laugarvatn, to Geysir, and then on to see the Hvitá roar over the Gullfoss. But there they stop. They turn around. The road stops, and the track begins, north. The earth turns dark grey. To the west are the cones of Skjaldbreidur and Höldufell, one a shield volcano, the other tight, steep, assertive. The road must stay to the west of the Hvitá, much too powerful a river to ford. The land has gradually risen to 500 meters, and the track points to a pass between the huge Langjökull glacier and snow-topped Bláfell, 1207 meters. We stop at the pass, throw a stone on the troll-pile and look down on Hvitárvatn, motherlake of the Hvitá, fed by a tongue of ice from the glacier, Nordurjökull. Where the Hvitá begins, a construction crew repairs a tiny bridge. We cross on foot, the driver takes the Bedford across alone. We will meet no one else for more than a hundred kilometers. Loury winds beat up from the south, spill down from Langjökull. The track leads through the Kjalhraun, an old lava field—bleak, dark, filled with twisted, startled rock. At one point, the Eyfirdingavegur branches off, noted on the map as an "Indistinct Path." It goes to the NE around Hofsjökull, the glacier to the right. Hofsjökull, like Langjökull, covers more than 2000 square kilometers. It is a trail for madmen. And it brings Eyvindar into the account.

.

The road swings to the west, climbs, drops a bit, and

steam rises in the sky from a dozen hot springs. This is Hveravellir. The wind is cold and spitting rain. We pitch our tents, eat, then, at midnight climb into a spring to soak. Some yards away is another spring, boiling, where Eyvindar cooked his mutton. He spent a year or so here, hiding, wandering, of all his years in the interior, wintering where nothing but lichens had wintered before. He and his wife, Halla, spent twenty years in outlawry, *úitilega,* life in the open. Two hundred years ago he built the walls that hold this spring's waters. Rebuilt since, I thank him, my head sticking out of the water, nose freezing, body hot and sleepy. In the bad winter months it must be a miracle of warmth. We run back to the tent, after dressing in the 0° C wind. Scotch, then sleep.

.

One day's travel.

.

The spoor of Eyvindur is everywhere in the highlands—at Herthubreith, in the Sprengisandur, in the lost valley, Thórisdalur. North of Hofsjökull a huge area—5000 square killometers—is named for him. *Eyvindarstadaheidi,* as empty of trails today as it was in his age.

.

Johann Sigurjónsson, who turned the tale he read in Jón Arnason's *Thjóthsögur og Aefintýri* (Leipzig, 1864-74), II, 243-251, into an immensely popular Icelandic play, wrote to his friend Pineau:

Pour pouvoir l'écrire en toute véridicité, j'ai parcouru à pied cinquante milles du nord au sud de l'Islande, donte à trente le travers le desert au milieu des glaciers où ejvind et sa femme ont vécu.

Here is part of his story, adapted from Magoun's Englishing in *PMLA* (1946), 269-92:

He is said to have pilfered cheese from a beggar-woman's bag and to have been at that time in Oddgeirsholar. She laid a spell on him that he should never stop stealing from then on. Then either Eyvindur or his people wanted to bribe the old woman into taking back her words; she said she couldn't do that, *because words mightn't be taken back,* but that she would remedy the matter to this extent, that he would never fall into the hands of the law. This point seemed to prove true ever afterwards in his case.

In many respects Halla seems to have been a poor lot: she was of harsh disposition, had a bad reputation, and was thought to be unorthodox in her faith so that she scarcely went to church or stood outside the church door while the service was going on. Her physical appearance and manner were described at the Parliament (at Thingvellir) in 1765: she was "short and lordotic, her face and hands very dark, hazel eyes with heavy eyebrows, adenoidal, long-faced, very ugly and ungainly, dark haired, with small thin hands, used a great deal of tobacco."

·

Eyvindur, on the other hand, was apparently very well endowed, of good and cheerful disposition, athletic, a good swimmer and glíma-wrestler, very swift of foot, and an excellent climber, so good at turning cartwheels that he out-sped the swiftest horses. That often turned to his advantage when he needed to save his life and was being pursued.

·

Eyvindur built himself a hut, and traces of it are still visible west of the Sprengisandur Route. The roofless walls of the hut have now almost entirely collapsed, but a spring runs out of it in three directions. The stream that runs out northwest is full of horse bones which had obviously been chopped up in meat, and some bones of birds; sheep bones have been found there. Eyvindur and Halla are said to have lived here the greater part of their outlaw life.

·

One Sunday in the summer when divine service was being held in Reykjaklith—the church stands somewhat away from the farm and is surrounded in every direction by lava-fields—Eyvindur asked to be allowed to attend services. He appeared to be a devout person; Halla paid no attention to the business. Permission was granted him. Eyvindur sat down in a pew near the door, and they thought it wouldn't be necessary to keep watch over him during the service; otherwise two men generally watched him. But while the minister was intoning the Gospel and everybody had their eyes on the latter and no one was looking at Eyvindur, he disappeared out of the church and wasn't searched for until the service was ended. But then a pitch-black fog came up suddenly, so that you could hardly tell one man from another. This fog lasted day in, day out for a week. Since that time Myvatn people call every pitch-black fog an "Eyvindur-fog."

.

A long search was made for Eyvindur and nothing came of it, but, as he himself afterward related, he hid in the lava-ridge next to the church while the search was at its height. Nobody thought of that, and they looked for a long time for what was right near them. The winter after he vanished from Reykjahlith, Eyvindur lived at Herthubreitharlindir and traces of his hut there are still to be seen. It is a stone enclosure, built up against the wall of a gorge, approximately a good six feet by three. He had a horse's spine as a ridge-pole in the hut, and a willow branch was pulled clear through the spine to hold it together; afterward it was thatched over with a layer of lyme-grass roots. In the doorway was a slab of stone as well fitted as if it were planed. A spring gushed out of the rock against which the hut was built and flowed down right past the bunk of the occupant. The spring was so skillfully contrived that one only had to reach out of his bunk, lift up a stone slab that covered the spring, and lower the vessel into it. A big heap of dry roots and branches was near the hut, and people think that Eyvindur kept his winter supplies in it. Eyvindur is reported to have said that that was the very worst winter he had while outlawed; there was nothing to eat but raw horse-meat and angelica roots, of which there is plenty at Herthubreitharlindir. Eyvindur is said to have stolen seven to nine horses from the Möthrudalsfjöll in the autumn, but there were a few sheep to be had in the vicinity.

.

After Eyvindur got back to the settlements he said that nowhere had he been better off as an outlaw than at Eyvindarver; for aside from the fact that he took sheep from the grazing lands, he had had lots of swans and geese there, running them down when they were moulting. Furthermore, he was able to avail himself there of the trout-fishing which is said to be inexhaustible in Veithivotn and Tungna-á, though these lakes were rather far off. However, Eyvindur said that the freezing cold winds on Sprengisandur were sometimes so severe that a man in his full vigor and well clad couldn't survive out of doors. Therefore it is more likely he said he wished no one so ill as to be able to wish him his life, than what he is also supposed to have said, namely, that he had no enemy so hated that he would want to direct him to the western desert, but that he would be willing to direct a friend to the eastern desert, east of Odathahraun.

II

Is the fact that someone genuinely thinks he means something a guarantee that there is something that he means?
Can whatever can be said at all be said clearly?
— *A Wittgenstein Workbook*

WE DO NOT mean the same thing even though we use the same words. We may know edges and similarities, odd coincidences. But the intelligence of deer trails is greater than that of the speech of man. Explanations are modes of imagining, as fortuitous and as limited as the shape of any stone, though not so easily explained. There is no fundamental mystery in a stone. A stone cannot cry out in some *planctus creaturatum*, in a lamentation of the fallen world. Its voice is soft and precise as an equation.

.

It is we strange wanderers who are the unknown variables of the desert. There is little sense in our coming, or in the paths we choose to follow. We confound the strict rationality of simple things. I say I have constructed my life out of chance and determination, and no one knows which is which.

My science, my one knowledge, is my own body—clumsy as a butterfly, and less hardy, but it possesses inherently the deviousness of water running over sand. By Arnafell south, as the Thjórsá gathers itself from the glacier, it does so by hundreds, thousands of rivulets, springs, seeps. Nothing stands still, ever. At the Thjórsá, one comes to understand the Herecleitian notion. And my poor body gathers in like a river growing the minutiae of the day, less for use than waste, but a progress of time. Certain hours in the desert walking are no more than sleep, and as rich in dreams. Because we are fallen? Do angels dream?

> After he had proceeded on his journey about five miles, by the way of an Indian trail leading in a southeasterly direction, he heard a queer noise in the woods off to one side of the trail, and being curious as to its cause, he proceeded to investigate and found it was caused by a flock of nearly three hundred wild turkeys that were fighting a terrible battle. He said he had never seen such a sight in his life....

This was in March, 1834, and the witness was Caleb Mercer, on his way to Bucyrus to enter the land he had located in Section 14 of Liberty Township, Wood County, Ohio. Mercer was a good walker, and made the trip to his home county. Columbiana, 200 miles away, five times, and the sixty-mile walk to Bucyrus six times. He'd generally take nine days for the 200-mile walk.

.

To the desert, open as light, I place in some counter-point of my own body, the forest, the limitless woods that stretch from Kiruna to Stockholm, standing, standing, citizens of some nearly immobile, no, *slow,* republic. The sound of low conversation in wind, different than desert sounds, where wind does not sift through trees, brushing leaves and needles, stirring itself, bubbling in sweet spheres of noise, but in the desert a slim hum across sand, imperceptible, over rock, brief and sharp. In the forest, sound comes from above, overhead; in desert, the ground is rubbed, and sound rises from the surface as heat bends light through air, mirage. Mirage of sound, soft or sharp, never muttered. In the forest, gossip, trees holding back vision, smothering clouds of brush and busyness, the horizon is indistinct as the future.

.

Light in woods is diffused, broken to rays, glints off leaves, there are shadows. In desert, light is as omnipresent as the sea. The sound of walking on stone, sand, gravel, contrast with the hollow humped echo of footsteps over humus, the ground a drum muted, absorptive. Sand *shushs shushs,* barely audible, as I have run in deserts, the *chunch* of my boots held a moment by the sand, pulling back, not wanting to release sound more than foot. Silence of rock climbing, of rubber on grit-free stone, wind-cleansed, a mating of surfaces, my sound my own breathing. I can walk more silently on stone than a deer, and more surely. For my pace on stone is naturally uneven, as the ground rises to my feet in languages, the sentences and paradigms come to the pure meaning of the shape our passage gives them. Forests tug and pull, always wanting to talk, social, gossiping.

.

In a forest of tall fir and pine beside the Imnaha, the wind pushing hard overhead, I heard and felt the roots of the trees pull and shift in response to the movement of trunk and branches. A presence announced itself to my dim perceptions: a language was being spoken beneath my feet. As I listened with my hands on the earth, I realized that my image of a tree—the crown its head, trunk its body, roots its feet stuck into earth—was purely anthropomorphic, and a reversal of the tree's probable orientation. The node of consciousness of a tree rests beneath the ground primarily, in its great roots and their tiny, sensitive extensions.

.

Those cells which provide consciousness require considerable longevity to function well. They cannot be shed or be subject to easy damage or loss. They require stability. No animal lodges its brain in its unprotected extremities; harsh, erratic movement disturbs consciousness. The seat of consciousness must be protected and relatively stable, for it is axis, viewpoint, source of orientation and identity.

.

The earth serves as a kind of skull for trees, protecting the roots, allowing them slow, steady growth. While leaves and branches toss and move in the air, the environment of the roots provides sufficient continuity for them to come to know the soil and neighboring roots with meditative thoroughness. The tree's focus of consciousness is in that dark soil, with its layers of humus, intermixed granules and stones, and sensitive to the quiet burrowings of earthworms and percolating water. It is attuned to the sway and pull of branches only as a man, wading a river, knows water's presence, though his eyes are on the far shore.

.

A tree communicates with other trees most intimately and enduringly beneath the ground, as rootlets touch, entwine, and stay. The flickering contacts leaves and branches have with one another in the wind are so random and fleeting that little of the order associated with consciousness could develop. A tree, I believe, knows what is happening to its extremities in air much as we know when our feet are cold or tired, but the world of the tree is primarily in soil, as our world is primarily in air, through which medium we focus our sense of sight, sound, and smell. Our viewpoints are contrary, and the order of a tree's perceptions quite alien to us. What's important to us goes on *up here,* what's important to a tree goes on generally down below, in a dense, hidden medium we inhabit only after death.

.

So the design of things, the desert, the forest, these patterns created by our presence in their processes, cycles, foldings.

.

I have learned walking that language does not break silence any more than I disturb a rock by stepping on it. I sleep on my own shadow each night to no complaint. I write—as I think all do, who take words as their métier—in spite of language. No word gives me what I want, nor is my way eased by syntactical patterns. Language is the hammer between man and a driven nail. It is a humble approximation of the way we would have trees grow to shelter us. I walk in a land above tree-line, my habitat as nude as a semi-colon.

.

May I come to *know* myself through language? Partially, I suppose, as it serves as matrix of certain of my thoughts. But language is more important (serving as that habit which will eventually be reified by a trail) as the vehicle by which I explain myself, most importantly as I understand *its* limits.

.

In the desert, the illegitimacy of certain questions is inescapable. That is, one comes to trust oneself. The strictures of the environment, the grammar a climber knows in leg, arms, balance, movement, enforce self-trust. Both style and necessity are as clear in a cliff face as in Cicero's *Rhetoric*. Moves, tropes, turnings.

.

I am not able to distinguish between a dancer's steps and an equation. Each depends on a space. Show me something that requires no space, and I will tell you the name of God. Unutterable.

.

And the connection between language and the world? It is not logical, it is ritual. *Use, not meaning.* My feet, the hut, hot tea, a coat. There is a knife blade, and there is the history of philosophy. One may cut a line, the other generate a circle. The names we choose to give things tell us nothing. But they instruct us in irony, and in the curious, pathetic circumstance of our consciousness.

.

The suicide of language is the desert, where the bowl of silence may be lifted, drained, and drowsy, felt-footed stumble begun once more to the mountains, beside springs, the golden plover calling us away from nest. from home, from swift return.

.

We do not know the source of the forms imposed on our perceptions. We do not know the origin of names.

.

So this: What *matters* has no intellectual base; therefore, the importance of walking. Walking reveals the conflicting will of God. (What God commands is Good. What does this mean?) Even a child knows there is no intellectual justification for morality. That it goes deeper than that...

.

It seems as though the very failure of language provides the only hope for morality. Dick Phillips, a walker, notes, *Compass deviation and local variation are far greater, and maps do not approach British standards. Rivers are formidable, and many old fords marked on maps are passable only by experts with good horses. Even smaller rivers vary, and having crossed it may not be possible to re-cross at another time or place. One must experience small swift rivers before attempting anything even moderately large. Little if any rock is sound enough for serious climbing. What looks like good fine running scree may be hard tuff with a single layer of granules on it, resembling a corrugated iron roof covered in ball bearings. Rockfall is common. Sandstorms can occur. Ground near boiling springs is sometimes unsafe. Ice-caps and glaciers are strictly only for those with relevant Alpine or comparable experience and equipment. Competent hillsmen who are aware of these points should not meet unexpected difficulties.*

.

I am old enough that I can feel gravity slope my skin away from the bones of my face, and my thoughts are scree. Walking the Kungsleden, I know my legs still hold, and what I need to dull my pain has not kept me from the mountains. If I can keep my life silly, innocent enough, I will cross different deserts, hills, walk canyons I have not yet dreamt of nor seen on maps.

.

Phillips mentions compass deviation. In Iceland I have

held a compass in my hand and watched the needle circle the rose, lazy as a bird, and never come to rest. That was near Hólmatungur, where the Jökulsá á Fjöllum cuts deep through the lava flows of the Hólsandur. Far underground, like roots in a dream, must be pipes of iron-heavy stone that makes a compass forget the long, steady pull from Bathurst Island under which the magnetic pole slowly travels northwest.

In the first section I mentioned throwing a rock on the troll-pile near Bláfell. Many such cairns are to be found over Iceland. Bored shepherds, road crews on a lunch-break, idle campers—it's fun to add a stone to a pile, or make a new one. On a small mountain I climbed south of Tungasfellsjökull, I found three cairns, none of them marking the highest point. Only once did I sense something sinister about a group of cairns, over in the Kjolur. Then much later I read in the *Landnámábok* (152, the story of Hallbjorn): "That's why there are three cairns on that hill, and five on the other." Each marked a man murdered. What was marked in the Kjolu, I do not know. But it was not happy.

Cairns have a subtle history in the arctic, and no one has completed their story yet. Two stone cairns on Washington Irving Island, in the Kane Basin between Ellesmere and Greenland, at about 78° N, found by Sir

George Nares in 1875, are believed of Norse origin. Men were sometimes buried in cairns before Christianity came to Iceland. Helge Ingstad gives this account of another set in his *Land Under the Pole Star*:

> In the summer of 1824 the Eskimo Pelimut found a little rune-stone (about 10 × 4 cm., or 3.9 × 1.5") on the island of Kingigtorssuaq (i.e. the Great Peak), a dozen miles north of the colony of Upernavik (75°57′–58° N.) The stone was lying on the ground beside an old cairn, most of which had collapsed, and had no doubt originally laid beside it. Close by were the remains of two other cairns. All three had stood on the bare top of the island which is something over 300 metres (984 ft.) high, and which commands an extensive view.
>
> This is the most northerly rune-stone ever found, and it proves conclusively that Norse Greenlanders penetrated something like 600 miles north of Vesterbygd. According to Magnus Olsen the inscription reads: "Erling Sigvatsson, Bjarne Tordsson and Eindride Oddson erected these cairns on the Saturday before Rogation Day, and runed well."
>
> Magnus Olsen deduces, from two of its own signs, that the inscription may date from 1333. The Saturday before Rogation Day was then April 24th, or, according to our Gregorian calendar, May 2nd. The inscription includes a number of mystical runes.
>
> What men raised these cairns, and why? Magnus Olsen emphasizes that the inscription was cut by someone well practised in such

work and that the spelling is surprisingly good. In this respect it may be ranked with a good medieval document. He regards the cairns and the inscription as a single unit: a memorial. The secret runes enjoin the cairns to stand fast upon the hill-top. Of the purpose of the cairns he says, among other things: "In ancient literature we read of cairns that were set up in memory of some event, such as a slaying or a fight, or to mark the spot for a future visit, or in a special way to testify that someone through perils and difficulties had made his way to a certain point. It is no doubt in this third manner that we should interpret the three cairns on Kingigtorssuaq." Yet they stand equally as a memorial of the most northerly point to which the Norse Greenlanders, of that generation at least, attained.

I add only the memory of *Inukshooks*, cairns "very like a person," with legs and upstretched arms erected in the Northwest Territories by the Inuit. They stand, dumb, threatening, warning, welcoming Hermes. Never fail to salute them.

.

Trolls, elves, and sprites abound in Iceland, and anyone sensitive to their presence notes this quickly. All over Iceland are *álagablettir*, or "enchanted spots" which are respected by whole communities. Should a public road be laid across such a space, there is great concern and strong reaction. I have no access to an etymological dictionary of Icelandic as I write, but

I would not be surprised that *blettir*, like our "bless," has its root in *blood*, or that *álaga* was related to *holy*. "Holy-blood-place." The old Icelandic religion called for outdoor *blót*, or "sacrifice" of a horse—a practice remembered in the Vedas.

.

This sacrifice is not required; all it does is mark an awareness and a greeting, even as Abraham discovered. Perception directed by will, and will by—what? Why do we walk? On walk, there are no teachers, no lovers, no such acts of commerce. There is only the land, the wind, the presences. Currents flow under the ground, and a walker knows their passage, their thrust. The senses we have no names for inform us most deeply. And as we know what our dreams are even though we do not remember them, so the awareness dwells: our bond to time and earth.

.

In certain places—and I know no rule by which they may be distinguished before they reveal themselves—the currents surge and peak, catching the walker, allowing him to witness the appearance of a pagan god. The place spills out of itself, and something *is*.

.

In the southeast of the Odadahraun is the great shield volcano, Trölladyngja, which rises only about 700 meters above the lava plain. But its rise and fall extends ten kilometers, like a slow and perfect breath being graphed. It is white in deepest summer, and traveling down through the black sands of the Sprengisandur, it is a long presence on the eastern horizon, a symmetry in a land more broken and twisted than any other. A great power lies under its snow.

.

It is not that there are beneficent or malignant powers, though there are. It is that the powers who find their location in stones, trees, waterfalls, odd winds, are powers of earth and of life. They are strangely shy, and nearly always silent. Though they are neither male nor female, I have found my way is to speak to them in the masculine, especially the guardians of *local* places, yet to think of them as I would a woman. Those who watch over whole mountains, and great stretches of land are profoundly female, reflections of Mater Tellus, and must be greeted and thanked with reverence and graciousness.

.

I tell you these things not out of foolishness, pretentiousness, nor as any kind of joke. I have walked much, and in many places. I have been in the presence of mysteries. At no place in this account will I knowingly deceive you. It is not possible for me to do so.

.

There is a word in Swedish, *trollbundna*, "Lapland madness" it's translated, *Lapplandsehnsucht*. But it must mean "troll-madness," for I felt that even in summer, the snow in patches, only the high mountains still heavy with white. The things that dwell in the earth, and their particular spots: *seides* is the Lapp word for such a place, a place proper to a particular spirit who guards it, watches over it. I know a stone by the East Fork of the Lostine whose permission should be sought before walking farther. Those ignorant of the power walk by, and are left to wander in the canyon as they may, like little children given the freedom of a strange house, but just to look. Those who stop, salute the guardian, and ask: they are given keys to all the cabinets, and their eyes will see as fully as their minds are prepared to comprehend, and a good wind will blow in the spaces hidden by their eyes.

.

Toward the end of my second day of walking south from Abisko, I stopped to rest and eat on a stone ledge that jutted out into the cold waters of Alesjaure. I washed my feet in the water, leaned back into my pack, face to the sun, and ate some chocolate. It was a time of sweet contentment, harmony, and peace. I could merge with rock or water, air, even the sun. The land was rich green, and in flower. I had stepped over some low-growing Lapp rhododendron to reach the ledge, and mixed in with it was *Arctostaphylos alpina*, which I had seen in Iceland, and is kin to our own manzanita. The little book of *Fjällflora* I carried lists 150 common plants of the arctic mountains, and it seemed that all bloomed on the hillside that swelled away from the lake's edge. Then I was given my gift by the troll.

.

Fifty feet to my left was another rock ledge, and washed up on it was a walking staff, just my length, sized to fit my grasp. I was far above the tree line, and the nearest beech groves were twenty miles away. Someone had cut it and used it, then discarded it. Something else brought it to me. I carried it all the days of my walking there, and blessed it thrice at river fordings, where it was a most necessary third leg, and then left it at the end of the trail, at Nikkaluokta, that another might receive the gift.

.

Trolls of the wild places are not to be feared; they are there because beauty must be loved, and always is. Things know themselves, and that knowledge is reflected in a way that we may grasp it. It is not exactly that the place creates the troll, but you may think that if it makes sense to you. It is not always necessary to be subtle, even when we know simplicity errs a trifle.

.

Receive the gift, and be thankful. Praise whatever is the giver. Be alert for the gift: most are never noticed. The Lapp shaman, the *noaid*, has a drum, as proper shamans must. As Shiva does. The drum is the world in time, and who holds it can walk the rainbow anywhere. *Die Zaubertrommel.* We who walk know the earth is a drum. Troll-madness is to so walk inside our bodies, in the blessed places. It is the madness of knowing as a chord, though we can speak but one word at a time.

III

In the old days men crossed the mountains on
foot if they had to travel between farms, and no
one thought much of it. —Haraldur J. Hamar

I HAVE HAD my heart turned as by a flower, a long
cloud heavy on the sky's rim, or the taut glance of a
woman, as by a crescent of land to the south of Hofsjökull that takes in the Kerlingarfjöll and the country
east to Arnarfell. It brings a twisting in my chest simul-
taneous with a glance from typewriter through window, onto a late winter lawn where two sparrows tit
and spatter in the dead leaves. Remembering that you
have forgotten something important, that you never
looked: that feeling.

.

Is there heal for these wounds? I don't know. The nest-
ing ground of the Pink-footed Goose is in the eastern
part, where the glacial melt collects, and the map shows
a little green. I like the names that bird carries: *Anser
brachyrhynchus* (which, if my Greek is right, means
something like "arm-snouted"), or simple *Heithagaes*
in Icelandic. They are grey, dark headed, with bright

pink feet, a pink band on their black bills. Big birds, like the Whooper Swan. Those I saw, stalked slowly and ineffectually, impatient with time one midnight, thinking I'd see others closer, but never did. I didn't know about the Pink-footed Goose then, and have yet to see one, though I did watch the Kerlingafjöll for a little while, coming north from Gullfoss, after passing Bláfell and Hvítárvatn. I didn't know what I was seeing, what was held in those mountains. Later I knew again how muddled my senses are, how ignorantly I must observe everything.

.

With eyes so hungry for what I was looking at, but not seeing, I watched pass by a tight range, a canyon there, Hveradalir, filled with hot springs; high about Snaekohlur a complex, tiny glacial system: twin peaks named Eyvindur and Halla (and over by Arnarfell, a fifty kilometer hike, the place they stayed longest those twenty years). The walk to Arnarfell is wet, through goose-country and ice-melt, river-beginning country. Bog-desert. Don't know why I'd want to slog through that except the good loneliness and silence. It is a sacramental loneliness the desert offers, cleansing, curing, wounding.

.

Perhaps that's why my eyes miss so much: seeing the desert is like grasping absolute historical continuity—a continuity that does not include human history, or anything human but foolish names on a map. There is time itself, not what we call history, *time*, in some slow and silent dialogue with water, stone, and air. Who can see that? It is created to be missed.

·

It is I who make important what I missed. Certainly I could find a hundred areas as large and tidily mysterious in Iceland as this place, and still know as certainly that I must walk there or die more foolish than I am today. Reasons do not describe my will. Matters of no matter gather themselves, and are a desert themselves (is that not a desert, that kind of emptiness?)

·

How should we spend our hours? What realize by them? How pay for them? These exchanges that never cease, the flux that holds us. My will for the desert is somehow keyed to a lean stride, an economy that rewards with largess of spirit, a true hunger years do not diminish. I watch a map, and my eyes move along ridges, cut the crown of watersheds, follow up-lift or intrusion, note the weathering drift of one land-form to another. I rejoice in ice, and the long breath of cold that sinks from glacier to the camp below late in the day. It is cold, moist air, with the smell of age to it.

·

There are so few to see, however long they watch. I think of the first loon blown from Newfoundland to Iceland. The desert is a confidence passed at night, close, but endless as the dark. A loon could find the cliffs and live, even return by the Gunnbjorn Skerries,

Greenland, across to home in Labrador. "On breeding grounds, weird yodeling calls and quavering laughter; at night or before a storm, a ringing *ha-oo-oo*." I've been an accidental most places I've ever stayed, a perigrine, riding thermals of will, scudding with downdrafts, hunting, traveling light. Better at just knowing where I am, vectoring, than why.

.

There is a paradigm that follows, not by force of logic, but that will I speak of—the will that has a rock right *there* and not somewhere else: Empires are to thwart time; a desert is a reservoir of time. An empire requires power not of itself; a desert's power is unalterable emptiness. Empires maintain armies out of fear for the king's castles. A desert welcomes an army to swallow it. A king needs quarries and mines to construct a castle. A wise man in the desert is surfeited by a single stone.

Why love the desert? For there inner form and outward appearance are the same, ragged and pure.

I am wild, and need to be brought up short. I am not myself among most people, and should not seek company, despite the loneliness. My family, and fewer friends than the fingers of a maimed hand—that is all

I should suffer myself. So the desert is luxury, where I need not hold back so hard, nor fail so regularly.

.

My mood is rash, more often than not, when faced with secular busyness, with getting and losing. I abide some necessity, by chance. But I do not understand how anyone owns anything at all, or comes to the notion. Possession is an unnatural state, and signals evil. As one given to following natural paths with more sense than most deer exact of themselves (since I am more clumsy than they, and must take greater care), I find nothing but grief expressed on land by a furrow, a road, the dark sore of a city. Still, I litter my life with things and markers, though I try hard to see they have little intrinsic value (as the phrase is) and can be misplaced easily. Cupidity is not a trait aroused much by desert dwelling, where, perhaps easier than elsewhere, we come to know there is no secret of the end this universe of matter seeks: one temperature is the aim of everything.

.

All matter will slip into the ultimate pit made by the merging of the last two black holes, so deep in strength that even space is absent. Perhaps that sullen, motionless thing is the egg from which the next universe will explode; perhaps it is just the last gathering, a waiting outside time. We know the particles that make our bodies were once in stars. So with all things.

.

My body burns as I remember this, and remember too

visions I have had explaining this course, demonstrating it within the bounds of my understanding, letting me see what was in my power to see. (For the chiefest vision is that one which compels the awareness of limit: Inspired, ecstatic, I am blind). So it is late in the evening, the sun ridge-running the Herthubreitharfjöll, alpenglow drawing the ochre to gold from the lava, I sit on a small ledge, the lava field around me undulating as the sea, and drift into the light as it breaks on corners, edges, plates of stone. But that I breathe, there were no air, the world was light and stone. A binary universe: where no stone, light; no light, stone. I, the observer, cradled in insulation, sit on stone, surrounded by light. I am the anomaly, the celebrant. The only possible liturgy is my simple presence, by which an *other* can be celebrated, joy made by the beholding.

> "...we do not enough conceive for ourselves that variegated mosaic of the world's surface which a bird sees in its migration, that difference between the district of the gentian and of the olive which the stork and the swallow see far off, as they lean upon the sirocco wind."
> —John Ruskin

I walk there, in a place where even a small noise outside the wind is an excitement, for the ground is covered by thick moss, and a footstep is soundless. I lean into the wind, shift my pack, and walk toward a notch on the horizon. I have not seen a bird for two days, and the wind is no sirocco.

·

I have decided I am walking across Iceland, north to south. The route is a simple one: from Akureyi, Iceland's second largest city, lying at the head of a fjord—the Eyjafjörthur. If you want to be punctillious, and start from the nothernmost piece of land close by, you must catch a ride to Grenivík, and then walk north along the Látrastrond to Gjögurtá, the head point of the peninsula. And then walk back. It's about a forty kilometer walk each way. But back at Grenivík, head south to Illugastathir, down the Fnjóskádalur, and stay to the west bank of the river. After about seven kilometers you will enter the Bleiksmyrardalur—a very long canyon running sixty kilometers due south. There are a few abandoned farmsteads early on, but soon even the trail disappears, and you must simply follow the canyon upstream. High cliffs run about fifty kilometers, then gentle out as the Fnjóská (that's the name of the river you're following) reaches back to its origins in the great beautiful wastes of the Sprengisandur. It is the most simple nowhere you can achieve by walking.

·

It's easy to follow the Fnjóská. You pick it up at about 200 meters elevation, and about seventy kilometers south, you emerge at 900 meters. The steep hillsides

out of the canyon are rimmed most of the way with basalt cliffs, broken occasionally by a creek, or, as at Hei-
mari Lambá and Freimari Lambá by lateral fractures in
the canyon's drive to the south. Freimari Lambá runs
about four kilometers to the east, and if you want to
come out of the canyon to the highlands, that's a way.
The highlands hover at one thousand meters there,
open, gentle desert with mountains far to the south
and east. Once away from the rim, the sense is of a vast
lunar plain, silent. It only seems more lonely than the
canyon, for there the sound of the water mixes with
the sound of wind, there are more birds, and the high
walls can be imagined as a protection. You are no less
alone in either place.

.

It was at that canyon edge that a vision caught in
words, and I added this to my notebook: "In the desert one may know that he has been the object of grace
from all eternity, and his own existence in such a wise
ennobles him in time before the universe itself. To be
more vasty than the whole reach of space, to antedate
creation! But these are the swift conclusions, easy as a
single pace, that desert engenders in a waking man." I
believe it still. There in the immensity, the words fresh,
it was yet easier. I crossed the creek at Freimari Lambá,
and walked on about two kilometers to the ruins of the
last deserted farmstead in the canyon, called Sindakot
on the map, and made camp.

.

It is late, and the alpenglow of midnight lights the eastern wall of the canyon. Contentment is being without law. Alone, the law is the heart *as it should be* with others. Thus the desert is Eden, a world uncorrupt except for time, which gives a frailty even to stone. But only in solitude are we released from the constraints of "the others" and may enjoy the salutary lawlessness we know as peace, or God. (The maps of Iceland tell the story: the *sýslumot*, or county boundaries, peter out in the interior. They disappear. There is no need for boundaries there.) The colors shift, a cloud moves, the water follows another law, and it is time for sleep. In a day and a half I will reach the end of the canyon, and then have about eighty kilometers of highland desert —the northern part of the Sprengisandur—to cover before the hut at Tómarsarhagi, and supplies.

.

In such a lost space, I turn to dream, and in my isolation hardly need to distinguish one flow from another. Sitting there the dream is as real as the lava beneath me. And so I sit here, the traffic outside an arterial pumping, downstairs muted TV, lean back to the cold of the chair, and am most desirably in Iceland. This body of mine is caving in. And the lies of the imagination I must counter each day are no dreams. Permit me dream, Sir! Permit me that faculty.

.

The aberrations of ordinary life, the dislocations of instinct and concern, discord, unhappiness, the shambles, the shards, the weariness of continual indecision are all mine, for I am Thursday's child, carrying a Ninevah passport, calling the litany of prisons, following the obedience of the fabric (Vionnet), and I, too, would as lief pray with Kit Smart as any man. That takes me back to the bar. It is March or so, the rain is furious with the city. Through the bar window (which is exactly, I notice now, the shape of the mirror above my desk) the rain drums as I have seen it in Mysore and El Paso. The physics are the same. George's son has joined the army. He writes encouraging letters about the hardiness he has developed. He may go Airborne. Five men are at the bar, one mentions the Round Table. Discussion. A wholly ignorant explanation (which is history) follows: it was in the Rose Room, the Oak Room, the Chinese Room. One man has never heard of it, and all the others explain, inaccurately. Everyone is too helpful. George tells them where it was, but bar customers get sucked into their own conversations, and no one is open to correction. The manners of drinkers are very plain. Nothing difficult can be dealt with, and finding a table back where it was once, which they've never seen and don't know anything about except it was there, even more difficult. Hand them a surveyor's transit, a log? Advise celestial navigation.

.

After the drunks left, it got a little more interesting. The rain died down. Rich fellow from Hawaii counseled that The Neurice Hotel in Mayfair was just OK and fine, but beyond my means. A long conversation followed on the correct pronunciation of names, and the group assembled did come up with some strange examples, as a class will do when called upon to recite Biblical verses, or lesser animals such as kinkajou or pangolin. It was 30 March, and the next night the Hawaiian fellow admired my Western hat, and we talked about ethnic dress. He was drinking brandy again. Think it was he who had said the night before, "When I run out of money, I just go home and sulk."

.

Next night a fellow at the bar talking horses, wearing boots, but he didn't seem to know all that much, and his hands looked soft. I thought of a boast I might make: first race between a quarter horse and a British vertical twin, 1950 Triumph, on the Rió Féliz, New Mexico. Instead, talked to myself about classified ads: "Genteel scholar, sometime Professor of Chiliastics, late bereft of employment, seeks same." He would collect chiefly rubies, I glaciers. Both unobtrusively.

.

Long weekends alone, hours of business, nothing of my own concern, then hours of silence. Sunday evening cross-streets empty as the hotel lobby. Dinner alone, no books, nor need of. Walk New York as insulated and silent as Lapland. The lines of buildings form odd cliffs with windows, shadows broken by footsteps. Walk. Eat in *Kitcho* cafe, no other customers, the two waitresses talking softly in Japanese. I have green tea and Kirin beer with my little steak. Everything good and quiet, comfortable within my taste.

.

George's lesson tonight is complex, and I am caught up remembering glaciers and dynamics of basalt. His theme is the thankless son, and simple: A police captain struck his son during a family argument. The son swore out a complaint. Warrant. The superiors were concerned about police brutality image so disciplined officer: suspended 30 days. He died soon thereafter of, as George said, "heart-break not heart attack." There is mournful affirmation from the gentlemen at the bar.

.

Once on the police, it is hard to stop: George tells about being mugged. There were two of them, with ice-picks. He gave up his money. Flagged cab, remembered no more money, but cabbie drove him to precinct station. Officers there (17th Precinct): "So what else is new? Why go out and get into trouble? Yeah, *those* two." Once George's wife, who is a nurse, took the car out. Thieves punched trunk latch, everything missing. Tools, tire. I hardly even want to tell you.

.

But late in an afternoon there, my gaffe. Talking with a gentleman about brandy, we are both on Couvoisier. A party which I think is out in the lobby orders brandy doped with menthe. I make a remark to the gentleman beside me about how thoughtlessly some people treat brandy, adding awful stuff to it. He monotone agrees.

Two minutes later waiter is back with glasses, asking for more menthe. Not enough. It is poured in front of my eyes. The people are in the barroom. I suppose they heard me. Deserved the put-down. Never looked to see who they might be. Feel bad for months.

.

Next trip or so, Lynn Redgrave is in the lobby, doing some film spot. She's tiny. I don't think she'd be interested in Iceland, and I'm certainly not going to ask her. Saw her outside in the street later, talking to two gents. Maybe, but it's not the place.

.

Each time I come to the City I become more confused. What do these people believe? What sends them into these dances, getting and keeping only what must be lost, yet ignoring the stone and metal wrought so incredibly for them? They seem affronted by the work of their own intelligence, yet compelled to that work. They create wonders—even useful wonders—but are disappointed in them, ill-served by them. What are their dreams? I don't understand. I don't understand what makes me such an alien in my own species, nor why I find such comfort in solitude and the desert. It is not simply to escape confusion, though I would see clearly, and understand. Something in the desert replenishes in me an energy and concern that is wasted by any prolonged contact with others. I do not know whether this is weakness or strength, clarity or confusion. That I do not know is itself unimportant. It is not a clue. What I do not understand is what sets me apart from my brothers, and lets me only pause and watch, never enter in.

.

"Remain professional and march toward the sound of fire," an old friend writes. About that time is time to notice that it is the karst formations of the Cassia Forest (Kweilin) that are the root of the Sung landscapes, and that the nearest living relatives of the birds are the crocodiles. Beyond that, there's only the happiness I felt, alone, carrying a paper bag with Coors and Dickle, eating a new peach, going west on Post Street! Joy like the Old Bastards, true and fleeting! Each morning in San Francisco up at six, out on the streets for an hour's walk, heavily backlighted photos of the East, and Alpenglow towards the West, if there were not haze, which there was. (I am imagining the ludicrousness of a highschool in which one may *go out* for Wisdom and get a Letter.)

.

Another, last bar, this taut, dark-hired, angry guy: "I listen to peoples problems." He says, "But I'd rather learn about snakes." Doomsday just 14 years, 4 days from today, according to Tony Shearer. Andy claims, "It is ALL in the stories." When you go on a walkabout, that's clear enough. The "Last great problem" syndrome collapses into the next step on a limestone desperate. It is comforting that all human activity is mysterious and not really to be explained or understood. In retrospect, it is clear that it is never possible to distinguish divine intervention from natural phenomena.

That I did not miss Mozart or Satie gave me thought, for music, theirs especially, sustains me when I am home and stayed from walking and its watching. But crossing the long reaches of the Sprengisandur or the Odathrahraun, an equivalent came from the air, the stones, the distances, the creak and heave of my pack and body. It arose in the muted sound of footsteps, and in the wind, whose regularity must be discovered beyond number. I see music more than hear it, and what I see are structures in the act of looking rather than golden pips lighting my way—and this has been my experience since I first went into the mountains. The shift in body's movement that comes with a pack taken up is a bass clef counterpoint to walking free of weight; add a staff, and a three point rhythm develops. On the level: *chunk-a click a chunk*. /oo/o/ And the small noises excite, draw one into the self. This is a grammar of walking I present you, not a guide, nor a travel book, but cautionary tales of structure in experience. Experience is simply the vehicle, as awareness is of knowledge in the joy and confirmations of oceanic consciousness. There is a deep health in feeling and knowing the root connections of things, the intricate mesh which has the ultimate unity of a point. I sequester myself from others both as a discipline and as a cure, for I find it hard to see with other people about with their distractions. But in the calm toil of walking alone I can measure the nearness of others fairly, and love them as I believe I should. As well, I am caught by the dignity and solitude of each *thing* in my presence, and share the simplicity of each in union.

The canyon called Blieksmyrardalur ends, and my steps carry me slowly up to the level of the Sprengisandur, about 950 meters. I don't want to risk a crossing of the Fnjóská alone, so I cut west up the last valleyside before two sharp, strange basalt cracks, unnamed, cut in from the west like slash marks. The geology of Iceland becomes quite mysterious any time a particular formation is considered, for the island is young, and built principally on the dynamics of vulcanism and accelerated plate tectonics. These are sufficiently obscure to make more or less learned conjecture a worthy source of opinion, and total ignorance an everyday companion. It's hard to remember an hour walking when my eyes or feet did not touch on some configuration as odd as a flight of albino bats.

.

The folds, buckles, and layering of a lava bed seem simple enough, but as that field is broken by newer streams and deeper flexings of the crust, the physical mutations of basalt take place, and the slow spin of temperature and pressure create gargoyle stones, crystalizations in half-minor keys, in what sometimes appear to be tossed salads of dark forms. In a young field—say the one at Askja that broke out in 1962—the pure dynamics of lava have not yet been touched by other processes, and the flakes and spines of stone are as delicate as fish scales, fins, or coral. Such new lava *is* as sharp as razors, and the crusty bubbles can give way to a footstep. It's worth a good many hours' extra walking to avoid such a field heavy with a pack, but you should take a little time to explore it as well, for it is a storm held in time for your inspection, a windburst of fluid stone, and you will not find its like in Kansas. Leave your pack where you'll find it, and wander a bit on stone clouds, bubbles of whipped knives.

My account is of observation, and whatever links it makes to what is, and the telling of the joy I find walking. As, in the lowlands, a hayfield wind-struck, the hay lodged in cowlicks, the paler green of the stalks' beginnings a yellow burn on the green. Such takes more careful harvesting, and there will be some loss.

.

Or in the moments of fear, in river crossings, or threading a path through a canyon of hot springs, uncertain where the ground will collapse, and send you into a sulphurous cauldron. Some river crossings are easily the equivalent of 5.9 climbs, or worse. And I do not consider a walking staff direct aid. The worst crossings are always tripled, for sense tells you to undertake the first crossing without a pack to find a way. Then it's back, and across once more with pack. In Lapland, to save weight, I crossed in stocking feet, and let the yeti know how I regretted leaving my ratty old espadrilles at home. If, at two and a half pounds, a pair of felt-soled canvas wading shoes are still too heavy, my old espadrilles, now felt-soled, are not. I carry 30 meters of 7mm Mammut nylon line out of a rock-climber's habit, believing someday I will encounter a terrifying steam crossing which will be made the easier by a hand line, and even the first crossing safer by a fixed belay. But I've yet to come across a place where the stream-bed and flow made a crossing possible, and also provided an anchor point for a line. It is a world without trees or even brush. (I once descended 70 feet into a cave in New Mexico, linked lassos hitched around a scragley sagebrush, and then, improbably, around the mid-girth of a burro. I was twelve at the time and believed that, if the sage gave way, the burro was too big to be pulled through the cave's entrance, which he was. Of course, being twelve (an age I've hardly exceeded), I hadn't quite realized if all my baleful thoughts had come to pass I might well be left suspended from the cork in the bottle.

·

Heights frighten me, though after some years climbing I know I can function well even though I am frightened. I just grow very cautious. And I have swum in enough bad rivers and surf to know that I'm not likely to kill myself out of foolishness. But crossing a rough stream on foot, alone, in the wilderness, with warmth, home and food compressed into a pack generates a special caution in me. I don't want to stumble and wet my gear, or be pulled down by it either, or lose it—a true disaster. I spend a long time looking at a possible ford, and will walk a good distance to avoid water deeper than a meter. To find a shallow ford, look for the wide spots, especially where there are small islands or bars. The same amount of water spread over a larger area is just naturally shallower with less current. This generally means you wade a hundred meters through water cold enough to make your knee-caps ache to get across a stream you might nearly have broad-jumped at another spot if you hadn't a pack on your back. The frigidity of arctic waters is real. No matter how warm the day, the water will be at most three or four degrees Celsius. A few exceptions can be found in Iceland, where hot springs running into a stream warm the water slightly. Of course, no example of this occurs at a place where one would wish to cross the stream. Toward the end of a long day of walking, at about the fourth stream crossing, pants still wet in a cold wind from a light mis-step on a previous crossing, one also comes to believe that a hitherto unknown natural law exists which places the sharpest and slickest stones on the ideal line of a fording. That is the time to start looking for a camp site and thinking of hot tea, or at least an occasion to break out the pint of Scotch for a swallow, and a few moments of contemplatory rest as much out of the wind as possible.

.

There is a certain blessing in fatigue, in the sweet, distant effort with which tasks are accomplished. All the moves of setting up a night's camp flow automatically, and my mind lulls itself with the routine, the learned choreography of tent, gear, supper. Even in wretched weather, once secured, the pelt of rain on the fly is pure mathematics, and body's ease both relief and accomplishment. In Lapland, after a hard 22 kilometer day from Alesjaure over Tjäktja Pass to Salka, I enjoyed cooking a great omelette to which I added my secret restorative—green chilis. It was the one can I permitted myself that trip, and after beating to windward over the pass following three river crossings, with two more to come, a bliss, for that day small angels hid in chilis for me, and music. Mexican chilis 200 kilometers north of the Arctic Circle in Sweden! From other times I remember the exquisite taste of six pieces of orange-slice candy I promised myself on topping out after bivouacing on an impossible slope in the Guadalupes. Dan Vickers and I had hiked the length of McKittrick Canyon that winter day, and had our own travails with ice-water passages and steep hillsides. We made the crest, looked back and down the miles we came, and ate the candy slowly, knowing profound satisfaction.

.

Summer nights in a tent near the Polar Circle, or north of it, are charmed in themselves by light. Even with a dark fly, and a grey storm out, there's always light to read by. If there was fear and exhaustion in the day, there is haven in the thin tent walls, and the words of Master Blake or Saint Paul to peal out in voices over the silence. The time I like best is at waking, when I can look out at what the day seems ready to provide—sun or storm—and in my ease make tea, stretch, awake, eat breakfast, and savor the fullness of the solitude permitted me by the sweep of land and sky that continues beyond my sight. Then I spend some moments with my old masters before I need gather my home on my back and begin another day's walk south.

.

The Sprengisandur would be called a desert even by one who believed no such things existed north of the Sahara. Black sand mixed with volcanic ash and dust-creamy pumice extends to the horizon, broken by peaks mottled with snowbanks, or perfectly white, as the glaciers, or the snow cap on the distant Trolladyngja. I've passed to the west of Bleiksmyrardrog, a warren of shallow canyons that lead into the long Bleiksmyrardalur, which I know now, and I have about forty kilometers across the open Sprengisandur before the hut at Tómasarhiagi. I hope a box of supplies will have been left for me there, as I planned. The great Hofs-jökull squats low and white to the southwest. Miklafell a high black notch against it. My course is ssw, and in ten kilometers or so I should intersect the four-wheel drive track. I can follow that south to the hut and beyond. The track, two ruts on the landscape, will be the first sign of other men I've seen since I left the ruins of the farmstead days ago. The country is wildly, crazily open. Due south I see the Tungnasfellsjökull, and I should reach the hut at its base in two days, or perhaps three if the winds are bad and I am lazy.

.

The desert harbors deep snow banks; the track is impassible even for Land Rovers till July, and the snows will close it in early September. But now the crust is firm enough for a walker, and no barrier at all.

The Apache Kid

I HAVE TWICE been on mysterious jungle treks that were finally as empty as dreams; if what we sought was found, I did not know it. The way was hard and long, and the goal obscure, or worse, never shared with me. There were good reasons, doubtless, I should be ignorant. Tactical reasons, security reasons, I did not complain, for who, engrossed in such a mystery, can complain? I would not have had the pleasure of the mystery had I complained. But the small way, however steep, that Charlie and I had to go to search out the grave of the Apache Kid, was as clear as the air over the San Mateos.

The place was known, at least to a few, perhaps. It was generally known, let us say. It was on Cyclone Saddle, a little to the NW from the trail coming up from Cold Spring Canyon, between Apache Kid Peak to SE and West Blue Mountain to NW. Some years past the grave was marked, but no longer. Somewhere I saw an old photo of the grave, a neat rectangle marking it out, and a headboard. The Forest Service says of old that there is a tree blazed with two old crosses near it. Charlie Mangus, David Burwell, and I had decided to rediscover the spot, and celebrate that old Apache spirit we would pay homage to, described by Ed Dorn with these words:

> The most absolute of the predatory tribes
> Apache policy was to extirpate
> Every trace of civilization
> From their province
>
> *Recollections of Gran Apacheria*

Massai, later known as the Apache Kid, was the son of White Cloud and Little Star, Chiricahua Apaches, and born at Mescal Mountain near Globe, Arizona. A member of Geronimo's band, he and his friend, Gray Lizard, escaped from the prison train carrying the Apaches to Florida after their surrender to General Crook in 1886. General Miles, in his *Personal Recollections*, remarks on their escape. He made the long journey home with Gray Lizard, who went on to Mescal Mountain. Massai paused long enough in the Mescalero area, at a spot called the Rinconada, to steal a woman, and then headed into the San Mateo range, just west of the Rio Grande at the northern end of the Jornada del Muerto. Exactly how he escaped from the prison train, and made the walk back without being seen, so far as we know, is an Apache secret, or as unknown a thing as how many breaths he took on any given day. It was not worth remarking on.

His wife told afterwards that at first he kept her chained, but not long. They raised five children in the San Mateos, and she said Massai was "not bloodthirsty.

He never killed anyone unless he was running short of ammunition or grub or needed a fresh horse, or something like that." At least, that's what Eugene Manlove Rhodes reports (*New Mexico Highway Journal*).

Massai escaped from the train in 1886. He got back in the San Mateos in 1887. He lived there close to twenty years. He was outside all law but his own for about as long as Eyvindur of Iceland was, and neither was the worse for it.

St. Augustine, quartered by Christianity, said, "Love, and do as you will," depending on love to give control. I don't know what Massai thought. He wanted to be free, and to live as he liked. He felt no need to love anyone who did not love him.

One version of the story has Massai picked up by Anglos as an infant, after a slaughter of Apaches in Skeleton Canyon, near Duncan, Arizona. This was Nana's band. The infant was fed burro milk, and raised by someone until he was sent east to an Indian School, where he perfected his English. In this story, he left school, bummed his way back, stole a wife, and went on as in the story. Annette Smith is telling this, and it can be found in *Chaparral Guide*. The Apache Kid would go to gambling halls to win money for his family, and sometimes people would be found dead in their cabins. Horses would be stolen. A man must do what a man must do, *nicht wahr?*

We drove the Jeep up White Mule Ridge to trail 87, not marked. But it was there. You can't miss a canyon that big. David was ill. He tried to walk in with his pack, but fell after two hundred yards, his legs giving out. We left him at the Jeep with a quart of Scotch, much water and food, and instructions to fight off the devils, no matter which direction they came from. Stay naked during the day, drink the Scotch, and we would be back on the morrow. Devils are everywhere. Charlie and I made a stumbling passage down the first quarter-mile of trail, which dropped from the ridge to the arroyo. Then we began a pleasant walk up the bottom of the canyon.

The trail was plain, but without sign of any passage. In three miles, as it narrowed and steepened, we walked quietly, and stopped when we heard a rock click on the hillside south. We looked up, and two mountain lions were bounding up the hillside to the crest. First time either of us had seen lion in the wild. They were yearlings and still hunting together. In a hundred yards, we kicked out a squad of mule deer from the brush, and they went clattering over the slope in their haste to escape. We had interrupted two lions' stalk for breakfast. Two more miles and we had come to such a narrowing of the canyon as to send us up the hillside in a series of switchbacks. We were at about 9000 feet, and I was breathing hard. Too many years at 600 feet. We decided to lay our big packs aside and continue with water and light gear only. This made the switchbacks easier, but they were still pitched at the angle of agony, and my method was will-over-sense: some few steps up, then rest, then some few more steps. I am old and wicked, and doubtless about 10,000 feet is my maximum without acclimatization. The col, Cyclone Saddle, was about that. Finally, we reached it. Beautiful ponderosa still, some aspen, and miles to see to the NE. I looked across the Jornada to the Oscuras, out of which such heavy storms had marched towards us two years before, as David and I walked the Jornada. A bit south were the San Andres, grey-brown and distant. I rested to find my breath and, after five minutes, began to amble through the trees in the saddle. This was an area of two or three acres, a rough park high up, with an Apache buried somewhere under the rock's skin. I could not imagine digging any grave here. If he were buried on this col, it would be only a foot or two down, and then be heaped with stones. He kept his wife and children nearby. They lived high to avoid those searching for missing horses, or out to avenge a death. Winters must have been very hard, even when they moved down in the canyons. It was more than two miles to the nearest spring, called on the map, "Twenty-five Yard Spring."

Henry Walter Hearn was in on the killing of the Apache Kid, and wrote up an account of it. In the December 1, 1988 edition of the *Magdalena Mountain Mail*, the tale was reprinted. Hearn says on September 4, 1906, Charles Anderson came by his place and asked him to help him to help tail someone who had broken into Charles' cabin, broke the dishes, slashed open the pillows, and left the place in a terrible mess. He had also stolen some horses. Hearn couldn't go that day, but four days later he met another of Charles' friends riding to get fresh horses for Charles. Harry James, and Jim Hiler Hearn came along then, and got Bill Keene and Charlie Yaples from the R bar R Ranch. They went by the Winston store to get some cheese, crackers, and sardines to take along, and he picked up his .30-30 Winchester and two .30-40s (probably 1895 Winchesters but perhaps Krags). Six of them rode out toward McClure's place at Poverty springs. The six split up, three going to Adobe Ranch, and Hearn and two others went to Sorrel's Ranch. There they found that Charles and his two friends had gone into the San Mateos. Cebe Sorrel went over to Adobe to fetch the other three, with word to meet at old Fort Ojo Caliente. About sundown, they finally spotted some sign on a faint old Indian trail. They followed it until they could no longer see. They unsaddled and lay with their heads and shoulders on the saddles, but did not sleep. All night long they watched a campfire in the distance. As soon as there was light enough to see by, they headed toward the fire. In about a half an hour they came upon Charlie's stolen horses. Bill Keene, Mike Sullivan, and Cebe Sorrel went ahead, leaving the others behind, watching the horses and keeping guard. The three came upon two Indians.

The first one was unarmed, carrying a rope; the second had a .30-40 rifle and a rawhide scabbard. They shot the first Indian, and when he went down they shot the second one. But then the second one jumped up, gave a war-whoop that could be heard a long distance, a bloodcurdling yell, and ran down the hillside on the San Marcial side. He left a blood trail, but they did not follow it. The dead Indian had three bullets in his heart.

There was a considerable reward for the Apache Kid, but the men did not claim it. Charles Anderson said, "We weren't just dead sure right then that it was the Kid we killed. Maybe we had killed some wandering Navaho. Uncle Sam had a way of a whole barrel of trouble for anybody that killed one of his Indians." John James made the gruesome suggestion that they cut off the Kid's trigger finger, but they just buried him there on the saddle.

The article goes on to say that a year later Tom Wilson and H. A. Faust opened the grave and took the skull to the Smithsonian Institute. It was identified as the Apache Kid's. How this was done is not reported. Some years after that George Messer of the Forest Service blazed the trees near the gravesite so it could be found again. The Apache Kid's wife stole a horse and rode to the Mescalero Reservation, and later her children were brought there. That is where Eve Ball interviewed Alberta Begay, the Kid's daughter, in the early fifties and included it in her *Indeh: An Apache Odyssey*.

Another twist in the story is given by Ball who quotes a letter from Mrs. Evelyn Dahl, "who carried out years of research on the Apache Kid," and relates that she had heard that the body was not buried at all, and Ed James, who caught up with the posse after the shooting, found Bill Keene boiling the Apache Kid's head in a vat. The Kid's family was hiding in the brush, says Alberta, and watched the men build a big fire. After they left, the Kid's wife went to examine the ashes, and found the Kid's belt buckle.

So perhaps what we look for is less than a grave, but a death site. An ash deposit and bits of bone, long blown away and ground into dust. After a half hour of wandering on the saddle I found what might have been a broken headboard, and some worked sticks that might have been posts for a small fence, and a long heap of stones about the size one would expect to cover a body. Charlie and I decided this was the place, and so we had a drink to Massai's memory, took a photograph, and turned back down the trail.

Jason Betinez, in his memoir *I Fought with Geronimo*, says the wounded Indian was Massai's son, who survived and fled with family across the Jornada and on to the Mescalero Reservation.

As with most histories, it is probably safe to say that if things didn't quite happen this way, they happened in some similar way, maybe. After the Indian's death, the problem with horse-stealing, cabin burglaries, and murders seemed to have stopped, so most people think it was the Apache Kid who was killed that day.

Whatever, Charlie and I can now point out where he just might be buried. The downhill walk was fast, and we decided to push on and get back to David and the Jeep to make sure he was OK. We had no need to camp for the night just yet, and so we pushed hard and covered ground. We were back before the sun went below the mountain ridge behind us, and found David working on the Scotch bottle, just about naked, and doubtless many dead devils out there in the bush. We rested a while, then drove out the ranch road to the highway and headed for a steak supper in San Antonio, there on the Rio Grande in the Bosque del Apache. The Bosque is a National Wildlife Refuge on the Rio Grande flyway, and thousands of birds stop by on their migrations, the thick woods entwined with old river channels, cattails, tamarisk, cottonwood, and the ghosts of many old Apache warriors who gather by the river to listen to the cries of the birds in the old language they remember.

Jornada del Muerto

I

*T*HE DESERT is austere and dignified. While a forest beckons and lures a wayfarer, the desert begins with reserve, with hesitation, and it is only after I have entered it fully again that I realize how much it covets my presence, how much it will possess me by offering those extreme gifts of silence, distance, and heat. In the northern reaches of the Jornada del Muerto in central New Mexico is a fine old lava bed, a Pleistocene *malpais*, and in the center rises the cone which fed the field. It was there that I began my walk of the Jornada. It was as if the Iceland I had wandered years ago had been continued at a different temperature, and the vastness of the Odadahraun, the grim eastern wasteland, was being repeated in the miles of nameless malpais before me. The cone was an echo of the Trolladyngya, the shield volcano, and the light flickering on the black lava in a heat shimmer something I had seen before in a rind of ice. The climb to the lip of the cone had been a refreshment, and the view south laid bare much of my route. I returned from the crest to my pack and headed south by southwest, maintaining the same angle of incidence to the distant Fra Cristobal range. I had ninety miles to walk.

With a pack I am content with three miles an hour, with time out for water and a rest. I carry six liters and will drink them all before nightfall. Two cups an hour, and more in the heat of the afternoon. The simple goals of the day are not to fall and break on the lava, to enjoy the heavy presence of the desert and the labor, and to find the cache of water and food some twenty-five miles away. The desert takes my water as easily as I breathe. If I do not replenish what it so effortlessly steals, I stay in the desert forever by tomorrow's night. That is the charm of the desert, as a delicate pitch on limestone is a charm that lures a climber on. To meet and dance, and to live to dance again. I am too old and clumsy to climb any longer, and so my dance must be a walk in lovely silence and bright, dry air.

Jornada del Muerto means 'the journey of a dead man,' and the journey of a dead man begins with one false step. On May 21, 1598, Oñate wrote "we buried Robledo," and the first European was buried on the Jornada. Robledo's error was not noted, for others stepped beside him and did not die. Death often chooses by indirection, in hidden interiors. Bad judgment, accident, the malignant will of others, or the inherent difficulty of the trail may lead to death. Some of these we can recognize and prepare for; others wait outside our will or anticipation. In the deserts I walk,

my mind may be set aswirl by the very silences and isolation I seek, and distance compound the complexity. I
walk alert, armed with the whole of experience which
has guided me there, and with desire.

I find in the quiet of the desert the richest ground
for unfettered speculation. Long views, and the pace of
a steady walk broken by pauses for rest or water set my
mind soaring in tranquility. The boundless spacious-
ness is like a music compounded of particular notes,
as the whole is filled with earth and air, plants and
animals, currents of wind, shifts in temperature, scents
here then gone, and the frangible crunch of footsteps
on sand or lava. There are times this music of entirety
is so intense I can in memory recreate every step taken
in the desert and mountains, and by some crystallizing
power retrace each path I have wandered, so rapt was
my attention to this music.

A step here, is a step there, in memory. This cholla
reminds me of the one on Cherry Flats, a hundred
miles east, which slammed into my hand as I carelessly
waved it from the pickup window, playing with air, and
catching spines. 1948. The black rattlesnake in the malpais lava mutes in an Ovidian change to the Western
diamondback Tom and I fought with axes on the banks
of the Rio Feliz. Every moment carries with it all our
past, and particular clues assert themselves, prompted
by the attention of the moment. But it is all there, at
every step. And since much of my memory is of others'
lives, they accompany me, a troop of ghosts—kin, old

friends, strange creatures glimpsed but once. A dead child, placed beside my bag in the Calcutta station. The astonished eyes of a man who wanted everything I had, including my life, as I shot straight through the burro he thought would shield him. My grandmother, roasting the skin off green chilis over a gas flame, talking, and scraping the skin.

There is no company so aswarm as solitude. You carry coiled in your body not only your family for generations uncounted, but all of life, spinning back in time like a cloud, coming finally to stem from one curious congregation of molecules which replicates itself, and begins the trek. Each one of us is a tribe in migration, the generations streaming behind fainter and fainter. Philip Coe, a fourteenth-century ancestor I know only by a paragraph, is there among the thousands and thousands of pages I once fixed my attention on, and kept some fragment of until today. People, books, boots, automobiles, jackets, all coalesce: the gestalt, the whole damn ball of wax that is the universe I know, follows me like a cloud. The Jornada ghosts I know, and figure to spot somewhere along the ninety miles, are the first two Europeans to die on the Jornada, even before Robledo—companions of Juan de Escobar. Nameless to me, they were sent south by Coronado in 1540 to scout the south flowing Rio Grande. They lost their horses while camped. Their companions pressed on, searching for water, and never returned. Those left behind looked for their horses and for water for three days. Two of them died, and the survivor, Juan de Escobar, stumbled on. Somewhere in the Jornada he was found by Indians who kept him, a curiosity more than a prisoner, for more than a year before he could escape and make his way to Mexico City. He arrived in 1542, months after Coronado.

Horseback, or pushing stock, or wagon-bound, the Jornada makes sense. It is flat and open where the river runs for a hundred miles to the west through country too mean and rough. But the Jornada generally has no water, and the ninety miles must be made swiftly, pushing everything beyond exhaustion. It is a place where you feel you could walk a thousand miles and still be in the same place. Enough have fallen on the way that the recorded deaths would require a grave every hundred yards. After Oñate buried Robledo by a small peak which he named in Robledo's honor, he pushed on north over half the Jornada, worried how his heavy wagons and hundreds of people and stock could make it through. He sent scouts ahead, and they reported they had found a stray dog, and with great joy encouraged it to go home. Home to water. The scouts followed the dog into a canyon in the mountains to the west, and found a spring they would call Ojo de Perrillo. A century later the band of Apaches which camped at the spring would be called the Perrillos. In the 19th century, Fort McRae would be built close by, but since 1916 the spring has been covered by the waters of Elephant Butte Lake. There is no spring on the Jornada now, but a few wells and catch basins, and dry lakes that are sometimes wet make cattle raising possible. The well water is alkaline, awful tasting brack. Creatures who had a choice would ignore it. Here cattle stand in queues before the troughs, patient as beggars.

I led my army of ghosts across the malpais, and into the sand, mile upon mile of quiet plod. Some people seem to regard my pleasure at such walks as odd, or at least suspect. But those are the ones who find their own pleasure sitting cheek by jowl with a multitude, watching play with a stick and ball. I too speak to those who cannot hear me, sometimes aloud. A tentative hop a few yards ahead caught my eye. A jackrabbit sat calmly on the sand, observing my progress with some disbelief. The antelope I had walked within thirty yards of earlier in the day had showed the same fearlessness at my approach. I don't believe these creatures had ever seen a man on foot before. Soon after breakfast I had walked by a badger hole and inside, its head clearly visible, the badger stared back at me. It was as if I were one of my own ghosts. That morning just before dawn I had walked some yards from my campsite to relieve myself, and as I stood, the ground around me covered with pieces of lava, I looked more closely at what I had believed to be just another bit of lava at my right foot. The dim light gradually revealed the sinuous curves of a rattler's body, tightly coiled, and the fine diamonds of its scales. I stepped a few paces away to finish my business. The snake did not move. It was waiting by a lava tumulus in which there were many rodent holes, and it expected breakfast soon. My presence did not impress it. This was the Jornada—aloof and indifferent to my species, a place where poetry disappears, and questions are immediate and brutal.

At one time I thought I walked the desert in search of some spiritual illumination, some insight that isolation and privation might bring, something of the motivation that led the Desert Fathers to their hermitages and to their austerities. But I could no more pray in a desert than I could in a church, and what little insight I had into the cosmos had seeped into my mind through the years, day by day, no matter how banal and boring a life I led those days. I came to know I walked the desert solely for pleasure. I took pleasure in the solitude, the quiet, the long views, the plants, the animals, the rocks, the landscape entire. I sometimes walked with a pleasant companion—David Burwell, a friend for forty years; Charlie Mangus, or Brian Richards. I am not a misanthrope completely.

Yet even with a companion, I spent most of the day alone. David and I always walked about a quarter-mile from each other, secure in ourselves. We met at water and rest stops, and camped at the same fire. We talk old times, or what the desert brought that day, and what it might tomorrow. From 1946 to 1951, when we both entered the Navy, we made dozens of desert walks, and climbed in all the mountains within 150 miles of El

Paso. David stayed in the Navy twenty years, retiring as a Chief Hospital Corpsman, and then worked nearly another twenty as a Physician's Assistant. We saw each other only once from 1973 until 1987, when we made our first walk of the Jornada. Time had not changed our temperament. We both walk for pleasure.

Three hawks rose from a clump of low mesquite bushes a hundred yards away, circling and keeing. They seemed worried at my approach, and appeared to be trying to lead me away from the mesquites. Between their own shrill cries I heard tinier cries, and decided they were fearful for their nestlings. I let them lead me away. A couple of days later, David and I found a single mesquite not over eight feet high—but the highest thing for some distance—with a hawk's nest in its top branches. We could see into the empty nest, but it was apparently safe from other predators. A hawk on the Jornada has a hard time finding any bush over eight feet tall. The one other creature which were cautious of man were the coyotes. We heard them near every night, but saw only one, which quickly darted into brush.

But water is a real issue. Like most desert rats we have drunk water of dubious parentage. At Fillmore Spring, in the Organs, we delighted for a long weekend from flow from a spring box in which, when we uncovered it out of curiosity, we found a dead rat floating. Not a tremor, not a gag, not a fever. Though with the spread of *giardia lamblia* by animals, I would no longer drink from wild water without treating it. Iodine crys-

tals do the job most efficiently. We had placed water
and food caches every twenty-five miles all the way up
the Jornada. It made something to get to before nightfall. That we also included a six-pack of beer and some
canned food which no fool would ever carry, but eat
and drink with delight if presented at supper, made the
discovery of the cache a pleasant task. Though the way
was long and hard, each day ended with a feast, which
our earlier desert wanderings had not always provided.
On one of our early trips we ran out of water and tried
to eat undercooked potatoes and drink juice from a
whang-leather tough barrel cactus, both unsuccessful
enterprises. We extended our personal knowledge of
dehydration on that walk. Our cry since then has been:
"Hydrate!!!" At every chance, with every ounce avail-
able. Put it into your skinbag, for water lasts longer in
you than it does in your waterbag. Drink, drink, drink.
Never leave a water source without over-indulging.
You will bless such excess later.

The way we walked, south from the malpais toward
Rincon, measures the true Jornada del Muerto, as it
goes from river's edge to return to river's edge. Millennia before the first Spaniard came north in 1598, this
had doubtless been the track. Folk coming down the
east slope of the Rockies, out of Canada and beyond,
picked up the valley of the Rio Grande, and followed
it through the northern reaches of the Chihuahua desert. The river is water. There is no other water. But at
the point now marked by the north limit of Elephant

Butte Lake today, the Rio enters a difficult canyon country, hard to traverse. To the east, on the east side of the Fra Cristobal and Caballos mountains, lies a bolson, a flat desert track which in ninety miles connects once again with the river. It is only ninety miles without water. It saves probably twice that number, plus ups and downs.

From the seventeenth century on, the Apaches were well aware of this. Until, say, 1886 and the surrender of Geronimo and his warriors, which put an end to Indian wars in this region, the Jornada was a deadly passage to attempt. Never mind no water. No Apaches made it a lark.

If Cabeza de Vaca made it as far as the Mesilla Valley on the Rio Grande north of El Paso during his wanderings, he was the first European to obtain a view of the southern edge of the Jornada, perhaps about 1540. Had he traversed it, he might have remembered it in his *Naufrágios*; but he crossed so many desert tracks, that the distant view of one he didn't have to cross could not have been important. In 1581, some Franciscan friars in search of the adventure to which they had dedicated their lives, following Coronado's rumors, came out of Mexico, picked up the Rio Grande south of El Paso, and followed it north. Having no wagons, the rough country to the west of the Caballos and Fra Cristobal ranges did not send them to the Jornada route; they picked their way up the river. Fray Augustin Ramirez, Fray Francisco López, Fray Juan de Santa María were

the religious involved. Francisco Sánchez, called Chamuscado, was commander of the small group of soldiers
who accompanied them. One of them, Hernando Gal-
legos, left an account of the expedition. The party went
as far north as present Bernalillo, searching for "Indians who had cotton, and made cloth with which they
clothed themselves." They saw buffalo east of the river.
Chamuscado was sixty at the time, and did not survive
the expedition; the friars, left behind to Christianize,
were killed by unimpressed Indians. A few soldiers returned and the Franciscans sent out another force to
rescue any friar who might still be alive.

The expedition of rescue was led by a Franciscan,
Fray Bernaldino Beltran, but the effort was financed
and equipped by Antonio de Espejo, who led the con-
tingent of soldiers. They, too, stuck close to the river
until they came to the region of the Pueblos, where
they turned west to Arizona, and returned east to pick
up the Pecos, and follow it south to Mexico. On their
travels, they did encounter a tribe who remembered
Cabeza de Vaca, and his companions Maldonado,
and the black, Esteban. But they did not taste of the
Jornada's delicate aridity.

After Escobar's vague wandering, it was to be Oñate
who first sampled the Jornada proper. Oñate's wife was
a grand-daughter of Cortez, and a great-grand-daugh-
ter of Montezuma. His own father founded Zacatecas.
Oñate was a true-born Conquistador. He started north
in 1598 with four hundred men, one hundred and

thirty of whom brought their families, eighty-three wagons, and seven thousand head of stock. He was almost continuously exploring until 1605, and covered all the ground seen by Coronado and Espejo, as well as much new country. When the expedition came to the rough canyons, scouts reported the only route for wagons lay east of the mountains, up the long, level trough which would be the place where the dead men walk.

The next day after turning away from the river, Onate made four leagues, found only a trace of water near some rocks, and so turned west, going through the divide between the Caballo and Fra Cristobal ranges toward the Rio Grande. A century later a German trader would die at the rocky place, and the campsite would be named El Cruz de Aleman, and Aleman it is today, a white sign and a small siding of the Atchison, Topeka, and the Santa Fe railroad. They abandoned their carts when they reached the Rio, and followed the rough terrain north. The main caravan continued north on the Jornada and reached the Rio Grande beyond the Fra Cristobal range. The first passage of a Spanish expedition was completed at the end of March, 1598.

Our first passage was in August, 1987. It was a summer in twenty, and the Jornada was green. Rain water from the almost daily downpours stood red and glistening in the bar ditch beside the road, and the cattle tanks were nearly full. Every plant was swollen with water and in the heat of the day there was enough moisture in the air that we sweated lightly. The sun drew back tons of water into the air during the day, and at dusk high thunderheads churned and split and the chabuscos emptied it back on the land with whipping wind. August is the rainy month in southern New Mexico, but we had not expected hours of beating rain. We had no tent because in all our years of wandering New Mexico deserts in all seasons, we had never needed a tent. David had a GI poncho, and I had a Mylar tarp. We rigged minimal shelters and took the rain like a lecture from an old Stoic philosopher. It could be worse. We saw not a one of the night-wandering wizards Heraclitus warned us about.

The malpais at the north end of the Jornada, just east of the last northern slopes of the Fra Cristobal Range, sputtered out of a low crater about twenty million years ago, and spread over about a hundred and fifty square miles like a great blob of black peanut butter which cooled to a sharp, Swiss cheese lava. The years had taken off the edge—the real razor edge I had seen and felt in recent Icelandic lava flows—and rounded it, gentled it. The desert winds had drifted sand particles, abraded and filled the rough landscape, and left a country easy enough to walk across, spotted with basins thick with grass. We had come in as far as a four-wheel drive could bring us, to a rancher's windmill and tank, five miles or so into the lava. A few head of curious cattle watched us unload our packs and extra water from Dick Inghraham's International Scout and wave goodbye.

Dick had driven us up from Las Cruces, up the dirt road that follows the AT&SF tracks from Rincon toward the ghost town of Engle. Every twenty-five miles we stopped and cached four gallons of water, and food behind some noteworthy scrub a distance from the road. David and I had ninety miles to walk with no sure supply of water, and we didn't relish trying to carry the amount we'd need.

But the malpais attracted us, as it would repel an ordinary traveler. There are surprises in lava beds for those willing to take the time to examine them. In Iceland, at Herthubreitharlindar, I had walked miles across lava beds that rolled like the ground swells I had sailed off California. Then there would be a break in the lava, a niche, a rift, a spring flowing, a single willow green against the black. And this malpais—on the topographic maps a mottled hachure that was the blur of the unknown and unseen—offered an invitation we could not resist.

I have never found it wise to camp too close to a water supply in the desert. Not that there is any danger, but creatures come in the night—cattle, horse, deer, antelope, and smaller things—and I do not sleep undisturbed. In Canyon de Chelley one night I was kept awake and most irritated by an asthmatic horse that grazed nearby, snorting, coughing, wheezing, choking. He was immune to rocks and curses. So we took our gear over a hillock of lava and found a hospitable declivity off the trail to water. Nothing kept us awake but the rain.

We had noticed an astonishing number of millipedes in the malpais when we first arrived, and as we wandered the next morning, it seemed as though there were a fat, six-inch millipede every ten feet or so. I have no idea what millipedes eat, but there must have been plenty of it in the malpais, and music to breed by. Small black lizards and black horned toads were everywhere, all adopting the color of the lava.

The antelope were still dun, and their tails still flashed white. They range too widely to adapt to such a local coloration. But they were more unaffected by our presence than any antelope I have ever encountered. It was as if they had never seen men afoot before, and considered us some new kind of cattle. We approached within fifty yards of a herd of eight. They stared, moved tentatively to one side, then began to graze again. Never before had I gotten within two hundred yards of antelope before they bolted with their amazing speed.

We walked inward, toward the crater, which rose a couple of hundred feet above the malpais. 5136' says the map, above a lava bed of 4800' to 4900'. There's no benchmark there, as even the saints of the Geological Survey will use an indirect method on a place that unimportant and of such tedium of approach. How many had ever clambered to the summit? A lunatic Apache, a bored cowboy, nobody ever. There's no way to calculate the answer. It is not a good observation point, so cancel Apaches. It is far, far from a cattle range, so cancel the cowboy. No prospector ever wasted his time in basalt, though I have found, from Alaska to Burma, that prospectors are the most indefatigable of pokers into odd corners that exist. I think it's likely no one has ever been there. We relinquished the honor after gazing over the seried steps of lava we must traverse, then considering the return plus five more miles to our first water cache. The day was hot, and the thunderheads of evening had not yet formed. There is nothing like the consideration of water to straighten one's path.

We wandered back toward the Jornada, which skirted the Fra Cristobal just at the leveling of the terrain, and by the heat of the day we had made the abandoned rail station of Lava, New Mexico. Here were the remains of cattle pens and loading dock, from the days not too long ago when one saw cattle cars on the railroad. The station house itself consisted of six rooms, each with a stove, made of brick and plaster, with a long porch on the eastern exposure. There was a concrete cistern in front of the station, full of debris and a bit of water. I don't know how it was fed. Perhaps through a leach field. The house was in ruins. No roof, most walls broached, but the concrete porch was a pleasant dining table and resting spot. Dick had cached three gallons of water there, and David and I sat, after about fifteen miles of malpais, removed our boots, and let our toes take in the sun. After forty years of friendship our vocabulary is tidy, and desert air precludes long speeches anyway. "Hydrate," one says, and we stop for water. "Gorp," one says, and we nibble our mix. Actually, we do not even speak these words, as we walk about a quarter of a mile apart, and drink and nibble at our own commands. But once an hour we stop together for a rest, and pass a few observations, perhaps say the words.

While we rested at Lava, more than twenty-five miles from the ghost town of Engle and the ranch with vineyards there, we were surprised to see two men walk along the railroad tracks in front of us. "*¡Hola!*" I cried. "*¿Como estan? Tienen habre? Tienen sed?*" The answer was "*Si.*" I motioned them over, and a man about forty and his son about fifteen, paisanos from deep in Mexico, came to stand before us. In the conversation which followed, I found that they had come up from a village in Jalisco, promised a job by a *patron* in San Antonio, a small town on the Rio Grande some thirty-five miles north, and on reaching the border had not been able to obtain green cards for legal entry. So they had swum the Rio Grande above El Paso, and struck out north, following the railroad tracks. They now had walked one hundred and forty miles. I asked if they had food. The father showed me some tattered tortillas. They had had a dozen when they began. Water? They each carried a two-liter Pepsi bottle tied with a rope loop for their shoulder. Luckily the Jornada had been wet, as David and I found we needed to drink about six liters a day. We could have done with less, and often had in the past, but two liters and the miles they made would have been a punishment. We opened some cans of food from the cache Dick had left us, and let them feast. Never has fruit cocktail been such a human delight. Nor green beans. The father wore Adidas soccer shoes, and the distinctive nubs on the sole showed up all along our path south. The father spoke formally, standing, with the beautiful manners one only sees in a stratified society. We parted with mutual benedictions, and they with a few cans of food for the morrow. David and I concluded that our trek of ninety miles, with food and water cached along the way, was a petit bourgeois weekend, and something we should probably keep quiet about. The only virtue we had left was that we carried our own packs. And it had just been demonstrated to us that one needed no pack at all. May the spirit of Álvar Núñez Cabeza de Vaca strip us naked!

The siding and the old station house-hotel at Lava was at an old Spanish *paraje*, or campground. There were thirteen *parajes* on the Jornada, and Lava had once been Las Tusa, "the corncobb." It was the first stop south of Fra Cristobal and the beginning of the Jornada. Our cache of water was somewhere between Cruz de Anaya and Madrid, the next two *parajes* south. We shouldered our packs and headed toward the next water, which we could imagine was somewhere just over the southern horizon.

Before long, I was half a mile ahead of David, and I unfolded myself into the solitude, as I suppose he did. We never talked of what we thought about on those

hours of plod, only of odd and interesting things we
saw. On that stretch of desert I was charmed by the
lushness of the desert, and my memories of Southeast
Asia surfaced easily in the warm breeze. I could feel
my sweat, and pushed a big handkerchief up under
the back of my hatband to shield my neck, and absorb
some moisture. The gesture brought back the painful
humidity of an evening I spent around the campfire
of the Wa on some little Burmese tributary of the Me-
kong no one ever named for me nearly forty years ago.
The ghosts crowd in, listening, testing my memory. It
was February, 1954, and somewhere to the east of us
the Seige of Dienbienphu was in full sway, and the Viet
Minh were dragging artillery pieces through suppos-
edly impenetrable jungle and over impassable hills to
bring them to bear on the surprised and weary French.
But we could not hear the guns from here, nor would
we ever. The winds blew from our backs out towards
them a hundred or so miles away. We would not hear
the guns nor see one minion of their tireless revolution
in our search for slipper orchids, rare rhododendrons,
and information so diffuse as to be the simple echoes
of a language I could listen to only as one listens to
streams, or wind playing in the trees. The Wa cut heads.
At least some Wa did, and lined the paths of their gar-
dens with them. It was said to make the vegetables firm
and plentiful. These Wa seemed to have no interest in
my head, so perhaps they were of another and kindlier
persuasion. Cousin Ben, his face a mass of grizzled hair

and glinting eyeglasses, spoke with outlandish gestures in his hands, as though describing birds of a distant sea, and the elephant grasses waving over the Laotian plains. I cradled his Mannlicher comfortably on my shoulder and sipped my tea. I leaned into my pack, itself against a tree, a small and ineffectual barrier against crawling things which made each tree a highway. Tea was my main comfort on these nights —hot, aromatic, both soporific and stimulant combined, and laced with enough sugar to restore what the miles and heat of the day had taken, at least partly so. A bowl of rice, with what green delights our cook produced, perhaps a piece of fish, if the river had been willing, or a bite of mammal, specie never spoken. A pepper or two. Sauce I used sparing, for it was as ripe as cemetery drainage.

My job was to fetch and tote sparingly, without losing face, to hunt if I could promise not to get lost with some conviction, to help prepare plant specimens, but mostly to give Cousin Ben someone to talk English with, and kin, so talk could go beyond the banal to family tales. Ben was a puzzle I never solved: botanist, ethnographer, linguist, and Nosey Parker. We met no one he couldn't talk to, and about something they seemed to be interested in, though he swore he'd never been in this part of Burma before. I certainly hadn't, so what was I to say? Flowers were the big thing, but talk got more attention. We moved from settlement to settlement on the big river by local canoe, up a tributary a ways if the stories were good, and further up by foot to the mountains if the stories were very good indeed. We might have been taking the census, and perhaps we were, Ben was so careful of the stories about flowers and what all.

We had encountered the Wa on the trail in late afternoon, and were camping together out of mutual curiosity and ease. They knew Ben, or of him. They liked his Camel cigarettes, and English tea, and like our *paisanos* of the morning, a change in diet for a meal. What remained in the memory most of all was the wordless pleasure of encounter, made the more precious by our isolation, and a human hunger for society. Perhaps that is what David and I felt when we halted our solitary walk and sat down to eat, and to search out a sleeping spot. In the jungle, it was hammock and mosquito netting, in the desert it was a patch of sand that looked a little softer than another, and an absence of ants. Then the rustle of grub. We both chose the most modest and economical of movement discipline in making a meal. I would open an MRE; but David, after twenty years of military service, including ten with the Marines, wanted no part of GI food. Rather a can of Dinty Moore stew, or baked beans, and a can of fruit cocktail. Sitting there as the sun set, I was as much in Burma forty years ago as in New Mexico at that instant. The tea was no different. Nor that I had walked clothed in a fascination all day, to become myself.

My troop of ghosts spread themselves across the plain much as the hundreds of Spaniards would have followed the ox carts and the driven herds of cattle and horses. Caravans frequently included five hundred civilians and half a hundred military, hundreds of cattle, and thousands of sheep. No wonder that the little water to be found was not enough. A caravan tried to make the ninety miles in three days, leaving Fra Cristobal *paraje* in the afternoon or early evening and pushing into the night, so that by noon the next day, the *Laguna del Muerto* might be reached, where a little water could be found after a rain. If there was no water in this sink, some might be found at *Ojo del Muerto*, a spring in the Fra Cristobals about five miles west. But this was a favorite spot for Apaches, and was always dangerous. Other water might be found at Cruz de Aleman, twenty miles farther south, but that would be the next day. *Ojo del Perrillo* also harbored Apaches, and was considerably off the route, so it was a long day beyond Aleman to the river either at San Diego, or Robledo, a bit further downstream. It was Hallenbeck I just remembered who calculated that if those who had died on the Jornada had been buried an equal distance apart, there would be a grave every hundred yards.

Whether the Apaches or thirst were the greater killer, I do not know. Thirst has been there since the end of the last Ice Age, some 18,000 years ago; the Apaches arrived only shortly before the Spaniards. Sixteenth century Spaniards called any wild, wandering tribe in the area *Querechos*, *Chichimecos*, or *Vaqueros*, and it was Oñate who first used the name *Apache*. They

offered trouble to the traveler from their arrival until
nearly the turn of the twentieth century. Geronimo
surrendered in 1886, and their power was broken, but
occasional depredation from bands in Mexico lasted
into the 'twenties along the border. The last Apache
outlaw, The Apache Kid, was not killed until 1906.

The Athapaskan peoples drifted down the east
slope of the Rockies from the fourteenth century on.
The first wave of people who called themselves Dine
impacted on the Pueblo people about six hundred years
ago. The Pueblos fought them steadily, and eventually
imparted some of their own agricultural ways to the
newcomers, the *Apaches del Navajo*. They filtered into
Eastern New Mexico, and by the mid-seventeenth
century, west of the Rio Grande. They moved in small
bands, and a litany of their names reflects their variety
and presence—Perillos, Faraones, Natajes, Gilas, Sierra
Blanca, Jicarillas, Penxage, Lipan, Cuartelejas, Carlanas,
Padoucas, Achos, San Carlos, Lipiyuanes, Siete Rios,
Salineros, Mimbres, Mogollones, Mescaleros, Chirica-
huas, Ojos Calientes. They were superb guerrilla infantry, and formidable cavalry after they took up horses
in the late seventeenth century. But they were not a
cavalry force like the Comanches—"the greatest light
horse cavalry the world has ever seen," said that general.
But on foot, in their mountains and deserts, they were
more than a match for ten times their number.

By 1609, caravans of thirty-two mule-drawn wagons to re-supply the missions had begun to be sched-

uled every three years. Each wagon carried two tons of goods to the isolated troops and friars. On the return trip, the wagons carried hides, piñones, wool blankets, and any other commodity of value to the Spanish. It is in the Caravan records that the first mention of Apache raids is to be found. The Apaches were a growing threat all through the seventeenth century, and the Spaniards were generally inept in dealing with them. Early in that century they crossed over the Rio Grande, for Benavides found the Gila Apaches in place in 1626. The Apaches were moving west towards the Arizona border. They were still afoot, for though there were Spanish horses running wild around Santa Fe around 1630, there is no record of mounted Indians until 1660, just as no, or very few, firearms were found among the Indians until after the Pueblo Revolt of 1680. Spanish policy was to keep both horses and guns out of native hands. But for about two hundred years, Apaches roamed widely in New Mexico, Arizona, Chihuahua, and Sonora, raising whatever hell they wished.

I have always admired bloodthirsty savages of whatever name, for it always turns out their depredations are far lest severe than those of civilized peoples. Apaches were terribly cruel and equally brave, and if they killed people, stole horses, and burned buildings, that was generally far less a burden than the legislatures of the several states imposed on their own citizens, one way or another. But camping tonight a few miles from *Ojo de Muerto*—the spring of the dead—I am just as content that the Apaches today are as bourgeois as the horse-traders of the Camargue.

David and I watch the north sky darken and boil, and storms roar out of the San Mateo, northwest, and the Oscuras, northeast, simultaneously. Something dark is also approaching from the south. Bolts of lightning tall as the Sears Tower strike down, and the rain, which began as a steady beat, turns up to roar. David and I sit on our sleeping mats, tarps over our heads, and watch the water rise on the desert floor an inch, an inch and a half, before it sinks into the sand. One stupendous crash of lightning and thunder simultaneously slaps the ground about a hundred yards away. It is a full broadside from all the 16 inchers carried by this cloud, and leaves us white-faced, grinning in the strange light, howling like banshees in a nether joy. Such a visit of elementals! Such a benediction! I want to think the Jornada del Muerto is as pleased with our temerity as we are. It was about here, in miserable weather, that General Otermin had paused in his retreat from Santa Fe, and all northern New Mexico, after the surprising rebellion of the Pueblos in 1680. Twenty-five hundred survivors had fled south after the uprising, with little chance to prepare for the ordeal of the Jornada. Little water, little firewood, no food, but much misery. When he tried to re-take the north the next year, he pushed his troops north up the Jornada; then, in defeat, they made their way back again in January of 1682, in cold weather, the Jornada covered with snow. Misery was a constant on the Jornada.

David and I lay back on our pads after the worst of the thunder and lightning had passed, arranged our tarps as we could, and slept in the rain. I awoke damp, gritty, warm, to sunshine, and a small herd of antelope grazing nearby.

II

A DAY OPENS like a flower in the silence of the desert, and before the heat shimmer begins, the clarity of the morning is as absolute as my eyes can accommodate. It is the hour to glass the mountains and peer with eight power at the distant windmill and tank and burst of greener green like a halo-dot around it. The mountains are too far away for deer to be seen, or desert mountain sheep. Ranging hawks pass across my field of view, and in the sparse, mesquite-dotted stretch before me are a few cattle grazing, and antelope at their ease. Who watches me I do not know, but certainly eyes and noses and sharper ears even in youth are well aware of my presence. David stirs under his blanket as I announce that water is boiling for coffee, tea, and oatmeal. My usual breakfast is instant oatmeal mixed with powdered milk plus raisins and dried apricots. Pour it in, stir it up, and let it set till the raisins swell. Morning Thunder tea and a nip of Wild Turkey makes me remember I am doing all of this for pure pleasure. Not so General don Diego de Vargas, who led an army north after the Pueblo Uprising to make a re-conquest. On December 16, 1692, he encountered Apaches north of Robledo, and in a short battle killed one. Some on horses fled. This was the first notice of Apaches on horseback. I saw no horses grazing when I glassed, but most horses are pastured near the ranch house, for simple convenience, and the nearest ranch house was at least ten miles to the southwest, close on the Fra Cristobal.

The sand of the Jornada is that lovely dusky yellow rose mustard brown with a touch of grey sometimes that characterizes the Chihuahua desert of southern New Mexico and west Texas. I grew up with that color dominating the foreground, while the distant mountains were dark purple brown steel, some more than others. Cerro Alto, in the Huecos, was Colt Royal Blue on the eastern horizon from my home. Colors like plainsong, a chorus to the eyes. Filled with colors, and oatmeal, I made my pack ready for the day's walk. My sleeping bag was an Army poncho liner, sewn bottom and side, and less than a pound; my tarp was lighter. The pad was a bit more. I had eaten the MRE for supper, so one pound the less, and drunk two liters. I had four to carry to this day's cache. Medicals, toiletries, extra socks, my "go-for-a-walk" pistol, a Ruger Single Six in .32 Magnum with 20 rounds, and that was about it. Water was the biggest part of the load, and I would be reducing that steadily through the day. As always, I resolved next time to travel lighter. But I had always done that, to little avail. Modest comfort for an old man on the trail demanded toting 35-40 pounds, with water. A Pepsi bottle and a dozen tortillas were more Spartan than I had in mind for pleasure.

Even more austere, however, were the conditions which George Wilkins Kendall faced in November, 1841. A member of the Santa Fe Expedition, which came to no good end quickly, he was taken prisoner and put on a forced march south. With great suffering, in cold weather, he and his companions marched the ninety miles of the Jornada in 40 hours, with four hours rest. The Commander of the Spanish troops, Salazar, was a harsh man, which is to say, an ordinary Spaniard of the time, and threatened those who fell behind with death, which was meted out at least once. Before Kendall, two other Americans had traversed the Jornada, with less duress. In 1839 Josiah Gregg, the indefatigable traveler, passed both north and south, noting the presence of Apaches in the Organ Mountains; and in the mid 'forties the Santa Fe trader James J. Webb made the trek. The English adventurer George F. Ruxton rode the Jornada in 1846, and in years after the American conquest of New Mexico, travelers were numerous. Ruxton accompanied Col. Doniphan and the Missouri Volunteers. Their train included the El Paso pioneer merchant Samuel Magoffin, and his wife Susan, whose diary of her journey is delightful. She was a woman of charm and courage. Ruxton thought that the "American can never be made a soldier; his constitution will not bear the restraint of discipline...." But he was proved quite wrong at the Battle of Brazitos, about seventy miles south of our campsite, and the acuity of British observations was once more put in doubt. Along with Doniphan went Dr. Adolph Wislinzenus, his regimental physician and a botanist who first described the large *echinocactus Wislineni*, and identified the ocotillo as *Fourqueria splendens*, flame-flowered.

By the next year, outlaws and renegades such as "Apache Jack" Gordon, made travel along the Jornada even more dangerous than before. The story of "Apache Jack" is rightly Wayne Austerman's to tell, for it is he who has done the research and published the results in *Password*. I recommend his article, and let me say only that "Apache Jack" was a bad-ass whiteman who ran with Apaches and delighted them with his appetite for their kind of cruelty. He was born in England in the 1820's, and was with Doniphan's Missouri Volunteers during the Mexican War. In 1847, he killed a civilian in El Paso and was courtmartialed. He fled, was captured by Apaches who were impressed by his demeanor, and, instead of killing him, they let him stay with the tribe and become a warrior. I wonder what it was he did that impressed them so. He led attacks on U.S. troops in Dog Canyon, over in the Guadalupes, and later at Pinos Altos. In November of 1849, he and some Apaches attacked a train of German immigrants northwest of El Paso. They killed seven, and took seventeen prisoners. The Mexican authorities refused to ransom the Germans, so the Apaches killed them, in Apache fashion. I will let the reader imagine what fashion that was, only to note that it involved fire, cactus, hot stones, sharp knives, and patience.

"Apache Jack" went off to California after that, and spent 1850 and '51 there; then he returned to El Paso, and gathered some like-minded whites to join with the Apaches for fun and profit. In April of 1851, fifteen warriors ambushed eight travelers on the Jornada del Muerto and killed one. In November, Apaches killed two herdsmen at Point of Rocks, at the southern terminus of the Jornada. On December 2, they killed Robert T. Brent, a territorial legislator, on the Jornada. The mail coach was attacked by forty Apaches at *Laguna del Muerto*, even though there were eleven soldiers of the 2nd Dragoons in escort. Four were killed, the soldiers retreated, and reported they saw "whitemen" with the Apaches. February saw another attack, with two killed, and then the mail coach again in March, and El Paso itself in April. A variety of depredations followed, and "Apache Jack" Gordon was last seen in the El Paso area in 1856. He returned to California, settled in Fresno county, prospered, and died peacefully in the 1870's. *Sic semper bandidos!*

As I have wandered the earth, I have searched out stories of bad men and law-breakers, and have always found them. Each age has a new name and a new explanation for them. I think the Hell's Angels had it right when they called such folk, including themselves, the one percent. I guess the rest of us are lucky when it is no more than one percent. Now all these statistics reflect attitudes among friends and kinsmen, remember. Apaches were kindly disposed and supportive among themselves, and Apache mothers and fathers took excellent care of their children, and were dutiful to their elders. But strangers and enemies could be treated with wonderful violence and ruthlessness. Sometimes. And sometimes not. It simply was wise not to depend on a friendly reception by Apaches. In the 1920's, when they stole horses from the Joys up on the Peñasco and Féliz, right at the southeastern border of the Mescalero reservation, my great-grandfather and his sons faced them down, and retrieved the horses without bloodshed.

David and I kicked sand on the remains of the campfire, and trod the embers down. There was nothing much to burn, but we kept to good habits. Our route followed close by the railbed of the AT&SF south beside the Fra Cristobals. After the lava field, we were on the Jornada proper now, with only much of the same to come. Mesquite, yucca, a circus of weeds, buffalo gourd on occasion, some clumps of Spanish Dagger, *lechuguilla*, in rocky spots, and then some more. Somewhere before Crockett siding, walking along the railbed, we found a desert tortoise between the rails, a prisoner of a jail with two steel walls a hundred and fifty miles long. We set him free. There were fewer millipedes than in the lava bed, but always the hawks, indicative of a healthy mice "and such small *tier*" population. We moved to the railbed when the pastures to the side, where the walking was much more pleasant, offered too many range cattle. We had no desire to have to run from, or at worst, try to shoot, an angry range cow or bull. Some of them could get downright territorial. A .32 Magnum is fine for jacks and coyotes, and even bandidos, but it is not much against a half-a-ton of mean cow. And then there are the explanations. The guilt. The money. It is amazing, how every trespasser that has to shoot a cow always manages to kill some breed stock worth *mucho*. And the courts agree.

Once I glanced back beyond David's following shape, and there was a ghost of a coyote observing us from the brush. At the turn of my head, the flicker of his disappearance was actuated, and by the time I had him in focus, he was gone. By such legerdemain the coyote flourishes even when hunted hard. Up on the Plains of Saint Augustine, some forty miles northwest beyond the San Mateos and Magdalenas, professional hunters took out nearly three hundred coyote in a month, and they were still plentiful, as the attenuated antelope herds of the Plains attest: few fawns reach adulthood of late. Even more cautious are mountain lions, and in all my wanderings it was only once, in a canyon in the San Mateos that Charlie Mangus and I heard a rock dislodged on the steep slope, glanced up and saw two young mountain lions bounding to the ridge, embarrassed at their clumsiness. The lions were young, twin cubs still hunting together. It would not be long before each went his own way over the five hundred square miles of the San Mateos, and on to other ranges if he wished. Lions are long rangers.

It was time for a water break, and I sought the shade of a mesquite while I waited for David. The temperature was about 95°F, with a little more felt humidity than usual because of the rains. I drank about 300 ml at each hour's stop, and was comfortable enough. The sun was high overhead, and I had draped a camouflage handkerchief on the back of my head and down my neck, á La Legion Etranger, held by my old Stetson. I wore some Army desert camo pants, a khaki shirt with long sleeves, and Browning leather boots over ragg wool socks. My pack was an Army Alice, and I did not think much of it. One of the shoulder straps had broken in the first mile, and this would be the last time I used an Army pack. My old REI pack, which I had carried in Iceland, Lapland, and Alaska was getting a bit old, but it would have been better. I remember seeing with horror as it came out of the luggage conveyer at the Seattle airport, drop onto the carousel, the ice axe popping the loop under the stress and tearing a pocket. Damn airlines. Damn the Army. Next time out I would have a decent pack. (I got a Lowe Morning Star which has been totally satisfactory anytime I need more than a day pack.)

David wandered over to the shade and told me of

a hawk's nest he had investigated, and the curious state of his feet, clad inexplicably in blisters. Twenty years a medical corpsman, ten of those years with the Marines, and he gets blisters! I chide him unmercifully, and we both dig through packs for moleskin and fresh socks. David is a sentimentalist, and accident prone, and a full accounting of his mishaps over the years would reveal only the bizarre nature of fate. He was always a better climber than I, and stronger, and more daring. I might have an edge in route-finding, and in the discipline of endurance, and I was lucky. Things did not fall on me, or me off things. I was seldom sickened by bad water or worse food, and I never got blisters. I sometimes lost toenails after long runs in my first years of doing marathons, but I had run sixty kilometers in one ultra with absolutely no damage. David tended his blisters with care, and voiced a long sermon on folly, and walking. He always did that. The more he complained, the better he liked it. This was his first return to the Southwest in more than thirty years, and, as it was to me, the desert was home to him. We both would rather die in the desert than anywhere else, and have our bones and flesh dry and sift into sand. We would be where we belonged. I have never wavered in my desire to feed the shabby, elegant turkey buzzard as a last gesture of acceptance. This is a fine universe and I would have no other, as I would not understand it at all.

Why it is that deserts have been so connected with the tomfoolery of religion I do not know, but it is probably due to common human weakness and city folk thrown into exile, or on a lark in search of ultimates and other foolish dreams. Already possessed of religious mania, I suppose a desert is as good a place as any for its working out, but I cannot think that religious mania is instigated by the desert itself. One may get a bit dizzy with heat and dehydration, or be scorpion bit, or snake, and hallucinate. Even bad water might bring on visions. But the desert is essentially clean, simple, pure, and uncomplicated, and totally devoid of metaphysics. I have read, and indeed, taught, most of the sacred texts of the world. I understand how human suffering seeks some answer. But I have never understood how such simple and obvious frauds so please the species. The absurdities of religion rival the beguiling seductions one sex employs on the other, but to no end save coin and power to the priest.

J. S. Haldane, being questioned about God, noted that God must love beetles very much, since He created over 60,000 species of them. All I can add is that it is clear He preferred elementary particles above all else, for He chose them for his building blocks. And what is that to a mother mourning a child's death? In the desert, God is dehydration, and ultimate ionic chaos. The human is a delicate chemical process, akin to making both bread and whisky in the same vat, along with cheese and blood. All the recipes sour with the wrong proportion of water. Thinking goes, and the senses (no wonder the religious love the effects of desert), and a horrifying confusion. Water is the only source of order. Water is order. Atheistic order. Remember this, and tell it to your children: Only the thirsty believe in God. Hydrate. The illusion will pass.

David has smoothed his socks on his feet, and fit them gingerly into his boots. The shade of the mesquite is threadbare, leaking sunshine. We drink a bit more before we shoulder our packs and head south. There is really no way to get lost on the Jornada unless one is raving. The highest peak of the Fra Cristobal range is now due west, and a few miles distant I see a windmill, a clump of green, and a small tank. It is off our route a mile, and we have no need of brackish water. Farther south is our cache, with good bottled water, some beer, some canned pears and peaches, sybaritic luxuries to lull the night into stories, if the rain holds off. There are no clouds now, only heat and bright sun, and more heat. I should have hired a servant to carry my pack, and another to carry a parasol, and a third yet, to walk for me. But I cannot afford such deviations, such insulators of pleasure. How, I imagine, can a great king or sultan ever enjoy himself, when he has so many subjects and courtiers and fops to enjoy life in his stead, so as to save him the trouble? God loves quarks and paupers.

Directly southeast of us, with the Gyp Hills slightly in the foreground, opens the notch of Rhodes canyon, home of the great American novelist, Eugene Manlove Rhodes, now too seldom read, except in his home country, where a caravan of civilian cars makes a pilgrimage

once a year to his grave site on his Bar Cross Ranch accompanied by a military escort. All of the San Andreas
range lies within White Sands Proving Grounds, and
casual visitors are discouraged. Rhodes Canyon leads all
the way through the range, and in the old days, before the
military occupation, one could travel from Hot Springs
on the Rio Grande to Engle, and then through the canyon all the way across the Tularosa basin to Carrizozo, at
the foot of the Sacramentos, and the forested expanses of
Lincoln County. This was the route of Apaches from the
old days, coming from the Mescalero country to sacred
places in the San Andres, and north to more spots in the
Oscuras. Salinas Peak and Guadalupe Peak were especially sacred to them. To the south, Funeral Peak was
the site of many Apache burials. They were everywhere
in this country, but left few marks. I imagine some of
their caches of dried food, ammunition, cloth, and skins
could still be found in the mountain caves, and bits of
mirrors on high points. They did not always use smoke
signals, but flashed signals as adroitly as the heliograph
companies of the U.S. Army.

When they roamed the Jornada, it might have been
safer for a single traveler or a very small company, to
travel by night, and hide in daylight. The Apache preferred not to travel or fight at night, believing, as Eve
Ball relates in *The Days of Victorio* that "he who kills at
night must walk in darkness through the Place of the
Dead." I don't know if that would have been enough,
for cutting sign was a high Apache art, and a hoof or

footprint is a flashing light to such trackers. One might as well travel wrapped in a bear skin, hoping that the Apache belief that bears were the homes of the spirits of the wicked dead and should never be killed except in self-defense, or even touched, might preserve one's life. Sweating as I am, there is a humor in imagining such a walk clad in bear skin.

The Jornada was such a vulnerable and fragile link in the transportation system from northern to southern New Mexico that it was one of the first roads improved by the Army engineers, in 1854. In 1855, Captain John Pope was sent to sink wells on the Jornada, hoping for artesian flow. And in 1857, Lt. Edward F. Beale led his caravan of camels in his extensive test of the beasts for the Cavalry. But these efforts did not end, or even blunt, the Apache threat. Fort McRae was placed in 1863 at Ojo de Perillo, but that did little good. That same year Lt. Bargie and the mail rider were killed at Point of Rocks, and in August the mail was attacked again. A party going to take the waters at Ojo Caliente over by the San Mateos was attacked by Mescaleros led by Chief Lorenzo on June 18, 1863, with two men killed and three women taken prisoner. Only one of the women lived, and who knows in what condition. In 1864, Capt. John Martin dug a well by hand at the paraje called Cruz de Aleman. The next year Fort Selden was manned by Buffalo soldiers, the black troopers of the 38th Infantry and 8th Cavalry. But it was not easy to pacify so much barren, difficult territory with forts every fifty or sixty miles. The road itself was the chief route north and south until 1929, when a paved road was opened on the west side of the river.

My own ghosts now were joined by the spirits of the place, and it seemed strange to walk in such an empty land and yet feel throngs about me. Lost, desperate, dying, proud, savage, fearful, contemptuous—whatever they were in life, they were all equal now, shades and wisps of imagination that played through my mind like dried leaves in a wind. We passed by the old siding called Crockett, a white sign by the railroad track all that was left. Back in 1917, say, when the Bar Cross was running 17,000 head of cattle on the Jornada, these sidings often boasted stores and saloons. Engle, with a population of a hundred or so, had three saloons and the Blue Goose brothel. Cutter, a bit further south, was famous for its Saturday night dances. But all was gone now, and the brief period of peaceful prosperity forgotten by most. The Jornada today is probably no more populated than it was in 1400, before the Apaches, before the Spanish.

Sometimes old ghosts leave solid reminders, and I wonder whatever happened to the Spanish armor Bennie Samiego found in a cave in the Caballo mountains back in 1941. The El Paso *Times* of July 14, 1941, reports the story of the old breastplate found in a cave in the Caballos. I have heard tales of numerous caves in the Caballos, and of local spelunkers full of experience and lore. I had caving days of my own, in the Guadalupes

150 miles southeast. David and Danny Vickers and I had explored New Cave in Slaughter Canyon, part of the complex of limestone caves that includes Carlsbad Caverns and the greatly mysterious Lechuguilla cave. We wandered a morning deep in the mountain with flashlights, and found wonders. Our lights held out, and in retrospect, that was the greatest wonder. Later on we investigated Goat Cave, and a few smaller, unnamed openings to the world below. We went everywhere one might go in the old Modoc mine in the Organs, where the largest single nugget of galena ever found was extracted in 1906—and shipped to Chicago on a flatbed rail car to entice investors. We poked around in the deserted gold mines at Orogrande, picking up fine specimens of pyrite and other glitteries. The gold was always gone before we got there. Once, in the Organs, walking in Fillmore Canyon, I heard the sound of a small engine, and followed the sound to one tent, an old man, a young man, a woman. They had a one-lung engine running, trying to pump water out of a shaft. They had discovered an old Spanish mine, and were trying to straighten and deepen it, but had hit water. The ore they gave me tested out about $100 a ton of mixed gold and silver. When I went back some weeks later, the camp was empty, the tent forlorn, and the water lapped in the shaft. They were also trespassing on Proving Ground land, and perhaps the Military Police had sent them away. I could hardly imagine an MP in Fillmore Canyon, though. I visited the site a few years ago—forty years after the encounter.

The water still laps in the shaft, and all signs of the camp-site have disappeared.

The main forage on the Jornada is black grama and tobosa grass. Good enough, but certainly sparse, and outsiders may wonder why anyone would even try to raise cattle in such pasturage. The answer, as always, is time and money. Those first in time to take an area choose the best land; late corners get what remains. Good land is gone first, and when sold, commands the best price. Poorer land goes for less, though more of it may be required to turn the same profit. Then one must add the complex variables of the cattle market, and true mystery reigns. The Bar Cross ran thousands of head of cattle on the Jornada and overgrazed it quickly. C. T. Tunney came in 1901 and bought up most of the land around the wells, and effectively con-trolled the Jornada till he was bought out in 1925 by Mr. Waggoner. Doubtless all these ranchers overgrazed their land. It was the custom then, and short-term economic goals often seem most important. By 1912, a presidential order established an experimental station on the southern part of the Jornada, some 200,000 acres to be used to understand the relationships of different grasses to varying grazing loads by different strains of cattle. The Jornada is fragile pasturage, and a delicate hand is needed to manage a ranch for the long term. Most of the Southwest bears the scars of heavy-handed management. When my great-grandmother came south by wagon from Las Vegas to Lincoln

County in 1880, she remembered the grass belly-high to the horses. Molly Mahill, newly married to Albert Coe, and accompanied by George Coe, also passed the burnt remains of a wagon, its driver killed by Apaches the day before. Some miles further on, forty Apaches on horseback followed them, waving whisky bottles, but did no more. They may have recognized the Coes, who had been in Lincoln County for more than a decade and were experienced in dealing with Indians. The grass was belly high.

Even in as wet an August as we walked, it was sparse and thin, and fetlock high. The cattle were sleek, but few: it takes thousands of acres to graze hundreds of cattle on desert like this, and the skillful movement of stock from one pasturage to another. Ranching is a balancing act, a complex equation with too many variables for comfort.

I asked David what he thought about while he walked. He smiled, and said "Nuttin." That was direct enough. He went on, "I just look at things, that's all." And that is the peace of desert walking. My ghosts, my fancies, evaporated every time I saw something that caught my interest. They were like clouds in the sky which can be stared at for long periods, but immediately disappear from concern when something else comes up. Something direct, something interesting: a lizard, a blooming cactus, an odd track. I think too much. It's been my business too long; I keep trying to mate words with experiences, align language with perceptions. Too busy. Better just to look at things and think of *nuttin*. Ah ha, my brain goes: D. T. Suzuki and the Zen Doctrine of No-Mind. And I am off again. Snyder reading his little "no mind, never matter; no matter, never mind" poem. It is to try to escape from this habit that I walk with such passion, exorcizing myself. I walk for that, but I also know I walk to tell about it, to put it to words, to make it an artifact that others can experience. That is who I am as well. It enters the equation, as complex as the grazing formula.

.

Today, a rancher can safely graze eight to ten cattle per section, that is, per square mile, 640 acres. The pasturage of the Jornada is in as good a shape as it has been for some years. Ken Valentine, who worked on the Jornada from the 'twenties till the early 'seventies, says he remembers before the drought of the 1930's being able to walk for miles and put each step on black grama grass. The Bar Cross indeed did run 17,000 head. But only for a short time. Such an arid climate does not permit grasses to replenish themselves to meet such a demand, and so the range deteriorates. With overgrazing comes the encroachment of creosote bush and mesquite—a phenomenon common in all the southwest. Little can be done to turn brush back. My friend, Drum Hadley, has ripped up acres of mesquite in one of his pastures, and doubtless grass will grow there now. But the cost is great. My own solution is to take on the patience of the earth, and view all our species' ends as short term and confused. Move into earth-time, in which the human plague is a few seconds ticking, and some equanimity can be found.

I found out today from Chris Allison, a range management specialist at New Mexico State University, that the mountain sheep herd in the San Andres—in the refuge established by Teddy Roosevelt in 1912, which last I had heard was doing well, at near the 400 count—had been hammered by scabies, and that less than one hundred were left. Some had been treated, and transferred to other ranges where scabies was not present—to the Peloncillos and the Big Hatchet mountains. But the mother herd was in sad shape. And he confirmed what Allyn Wasser, district ranger in the Forest Service at Magdalena, had told me a few years ago: that predators, especially coyotes, were wrecking havoc with the antelope and deer herds. One survey of fawns up north with radio collars had shown that 80% were killed by coyotes before their first winter. I like coyotes, just as I like savages, but when it comes to living with them, you've got to learn how to keep them in their place.

.

We have passed Crockett, and come to the place where the high tension line cuts southeast. It will intersect the old road, and there lies our cache for tonight. David's blisters are worse, and he is on a long retreat from some Moscow of the lava beds, some Chonjin Reservoir of sand. Each step is hard. And painful. And there is no way out, no help to call for. The land rises by some fifty feet, slowly, but really. Mesquite and looser sand, as the desert nears El Paso, become the norm: it is redder here. It is also high afternoon, and as hot as it will get. I do not carry a thermometer, considering that effete or otherwise disgusting. I do not carry a compass, either, as I damn well know which way is north or south or in between. I do carry a compass in deep flat woods, when I can be induced to walk in them. By this time I am a mile or so in front of David, and come to the cache we laid. I rest, leave my pack, and take up two cans of warm beer and strike back on the trail. The less David complains, the more I know he hurts. I find him, we drink, and proceed towards the campsite for tonight. There are many ants on the ground, so we move a hundred yards to a flat, smooth piece of desert and begin our preparations for the night. All around, the clouds boil up again in storm. While we have sun, in every direction dark clouds threaten. Soon, the sun is set behind a bank of black roiling clouds. The lightning strokes begin to the east-northeast, once more from the Oscuras, another group responds. The clouds rush at us, and in the south the thunderheads boil up higher than the jet-trails of the airliners going in to El Paso, some 120 miles away. For a simple place, this desert has become complex, and the sky as threatening as a compound of air and water can be. The clouds move toward us from all directions, as though we were the focus of their attention, the very center of some vortex calling them. They came, and spoke to us for hours, punctuating their eloquence with lightning strokes and thunder.

Such was the third night, after walking about fifty miles. We were about ten miles north of Engle, where two families actually lived, and would pass by some few hundred acres of vinyards on our way there. We had been surprised to see them on the way north in Dick's Scout, and he explained that the wine industry in southern New Mexico had grown a lot in the years we were away; there were vineyards near Deming, down by Las Cruces, and here on the Jornada. After a few miles of walking the next morning, we came to the first vineyards, each plant watered by a plastic tube, and before long passed a 24" pipe coming from the west, where Elephant Butte Lake was, some eight miles away. Later I made a visit to the winery, and had a pleasant tour from the resident winemaker, a young American. He told me there were four vineyards on the Jornada sharing the water: one German, one Swiss, and two French. This was the vineyard and winery of Robert Jacques Cherluin, and produced champagne, pinot noir, and chardonnay. Some tasting led to the purchase of several bottles of their champagne. But as David and I walked by, we could only dream of wine, and marvel. We saw no one, though some miles farther on we saw a freight train slow and stop at a siding, and we walked over to say hello. We must have been strange enough apparitions, but the engineer slid open his window six feet above us, leaned out, and said, "You boys look like you could use a little cold water," and dropped to me a six- pack of ice cold water bottles. It had never occurred to me that those huge locomotives had refrigerators— and one wonders what else—in their cabs. We praised him for his generosity and divvied up the six-pack. I noticed my three bottles were empty within a mile. Of water we had, if not plenty, enough; but cold water was something beyond a walker's dream on the Jornada.

David lagged farther behind, and his blisters grew worse. I did not see how he could continue for another forty or fifty miles. At Engle, State Road 52 comes in from Elephant Butte and Truth or Consequences. It is even paved. It is eleven miles to the dam, and four more to TorC. But I could walk in and rent a car and come back for David if need be. A little before noon I ambled in to Engle, with its two occupied houses, and an old rock school house with a sign in front of it reading, "Engle Country Church." A man working on a railway signal box looked up as I approached, and we spent a few minutes in conversation. A pleasant fellow. I put my pack down by the road, and wandered over to the Country Church. It had been built as a school when Engle was bustling as the rail station for all the construction materials, workers, supplies, and what-all during the construction of Elephant Butte dam back in 1911-1916.

Engle's beginning went back to 1880 and the construction of the railway. It had supplied the mining boom of '80-'83, and by 1896 it was a shipping center for cattle driven across from Lincoln county during the wet season. Then the dam came, but by 1920 Engle was finished as a town. From Engle south on the Jornada was a real county road, graded and fairly fast, that paralleled the railroad down to Rincon. We had planned to walk beside it, occasionally cutting toward the Caballos as the terrain invited. But it did not look like we would make it this trip. David limped up to join me, the strain showing on his face. We decided to cut on 52 over to the dam, and if we could hitch a ride along the way, our honor would not be compromised. We started west, pavement strange underfoot after all the miles of desert, and two- to five-million-year-old lava belched out of the crater now below the northern horizon. We had walked a good piece—the best part of the Jornada. And another time we would finish off the southern portion.

A mile or so down 52, the pickup of the signal repairman stopped beside us, and he beckoned us to board. It was a welcome gesture. David climbed in back and lay down; I rode with the repairman and traded stories till we got to Truth or Consequences. I will not recount here the melancholy tale of how a town was seduced by greed to change its name from Hot Springs. The reader probably already knows, and one would not guess incorrectly. TorC is depressed, as are we all, and the community I remember from fishing trips with my father in the 40's is thin and grey and beaten. David and I found the Greyhound station, bought a ticket to

Las Cruces, and set out to find a congenial bar to wait in. There are several in TorC. As we sat, drinks cold in the hand, we figured we had walked forty-five miles, maybe fifty. We still had a few days before we must leave, and we planned to do what we could that did not involve too many more miles on David's feet.

.

By mid-afternoon we were in Las Cruces, and I called the Ingrahams to tell them we were back two days early. Elena picked us up at the station, and brought us to their place The idea of a hot shower and a change of clothes, another drink or two, and a good dinner, on us, seemed appropriate. And so we did, and told our tales of wonder and folly, and celebrated life.

David and I took the rental car, and used it as base for camps on the east and west side of the Organs—at Aguirre Springs, where we watched on sunset-time as golden eagles rose from the cliffs of the Organs, circling in the thermals, until there were sixteen of them aloft at once, and then, as the light grew more golden red, each slid on a long gliding flight over the crest of the Needles to hunt on the western slopes. And we camped near Rock House mine, a place we'd known forty years before, we listened to coyotes sing at the spectacle of the light stick we had tied to a mesquite limb as it gradually dimmed over the evening. We had visited Ciudad Juarez earlier that day, and David bought a scratchy Mexican blanket he rolled himself in. There were times we remembered when a sleeping bag, like a decent pack, was a luxury beyond us, and we slept on rock, curled in an army blanket, carried rolled over one shoulder, while on the other I hung my father's musette bag from his days—1929-30—as an officer in the National Guard. Lousy equipment never even slowed us down, for we were ignorant, young, and strong, and possessed by the desire to see what lay beyond the next ridge, or if there were a spring in that canyon where a bit of green seemed to show. There generally was not, for this is desert country, but there was always something at least as wonderful as a spring. After a life of this, I know where a number of such wonders can be found.

I left an army of ghosts on the Jornada, patient, dozing perhaps, and can call them back like trained smoke when I want. But most I leave there, where they belong. I have other ghosts for life in Ohio. Everywhere I've been. Spoor. A trail. Tracks. Sign. The signature of passage.

I have since returned three times, to lounge and wander, to poke around, to sit and look at distances I once walked, do walk, and will walk again. A lifetime of meditation has led me to believe that there is little that is better to do in this world, or more pleasurable, than to walk unfrequented places.

POSTSCRIPT FOR JENNIFER

A little bit of Scotch lying in wait at the bottom bell curve of a wine glass, a can of Molson Golden, and the false work of the week finished: it will be one week the less I pine for the desert.

My eyes fix on the hachures of a lava bed, and the thick contours that signal mountain no-man-trod this year. A floral carved Tom Threeperson cross-draw for my .45, newly arrived, waits like a passport for the traveler to employ properly by leaving town.

Choosing the right pistol can take a month, a fruitful month of time in the purgatory of gainful employment. The boots I already know, chosen of three pair; the thorn-proof pants, the hat, the shirt, the pack and water bottles, the single knife that always is for more than cutting, the tin Filson coat made sacred by fifteen years or more: ikons of a wanderer.

Tonight the rain spits lightly, the dogs lounge in the garage, unwilling to get wet, but not interested in lying down before the fire. Squirrels still rummage in the leaves by day, and I killed six bloated, slow, November flies that lurched on the kitchen counters all afternoon. We are between seasons. Something is dying, but is not quite dead. Nothing waits its turn.

The thin layer of Scotch has disappeared in four stanzas, to be replaced by half an inch of Elijah Craig; the

Molson holds its own. The photographs of my wife, age 12, 18, and 24 gladden my heart, and I can watch them as I type, her eyes and smile as fixed and real as Plato's Forms. She is with me in the desert though she loves the sea.

The finest music is made by wind accompanied by rock, most sweetly on a ridge's edge that falls to either side like a falcon stooping to its prey. The nether notes lie far beyond the eyes' ability to see, and the nearest note is most unheard, like a bullet to the brain.

I have languages in me that have no name and are unspoke, but felt; numbers fill their dictionary, like a code engendered by the curve of my wife's lovely breasts. I miss her when I walk the hills, and wonder why I must so walk. Else I dry and mold, like bread left in a closet.

What can children understand of the joy they bring? It is unaccountable to such young minds. And there is no way possible to tell what lights my eyes, for I am not obvious for art. Indeed, I would not have them know until they are as old as I, and cunning in their sentiments.

The intellect betrays before the heart, as Elijah Craig well knew. Chip machines, light rulers, the glue of plasmas and imaginary strings infect my mind with sweet (I use the word again) delirium, and only the desert cures. I write one poem a year to keep me sane, or circumambulate an island range. Alamo Hueco. Guadalupes. Los Peloncillos. Jennifer.

SOURCES

Paul I. Wellman, *Death in the Desert*, NY: Pyramid Books, 1963.

Eugene Manlove Rhodes, "When Apache Kid Took A Wife," *New Mexico Highway Journal*, January, 1928, pp. 6-7.

Cleve Hallenbeck and Juanita H. Williams, *Legends of the Spanish Southwest*, Glendale: Arthur H. Clark, 1938.

Eve Ball, *Apache Odyssey*, Provo: BYU Press, 1980.

Jason Betzinez, *I Fought With Geronimo*, Stackpole, 1959.

Annette Smith, "Apache Kid Said To Have Been Cold, Calculating, Fearless," *Chaparral Guide*, Truth or Consequences, New Mexico, 1987

Henry Walter Hearn, "How Apache Kid Met Death," Magdalena *Mountain Mail*, Magdalena, NM, Vol. 9, #11, December 1, 1988.

George Wilkins Kendall, *Narrative of the Texas Santa Fe Expedition*, NY: Harpers, 1844.

Password, the Journal of the El Paso County Historical Society, Vol. XXXIII, #2, Summer 1988.

Albert Schroeder, *Apache Indians*, Garland, 1974.

Cleve Hallenbeck, *Land of the Conquistadores*, Caldwell: The Caxton Printers, 1950.

Edwin A. Tucker and George Fitzpatrick, *Men Who Matched the Mountains*, United States Department of Agriculture, 1972.

Ralph Emerson Twitchell, *Leading Facts in New Mexico History*, Cedar Rapids, 1912.

Wayne R. Austerman, "Apache Jack Gordon," *Password*, El Paso County Historical Society, 1988. Vol. 33, #2.

Jack D. Forbes, Apache, *Navaho and Spaniard*, Norman, Okla.: University of Oklahoma Press, 1960.

Susan Magoffin, *Down The Santa Fe Trail*, New Haven, Conn.: Yale, 1926.

Col. George Archibold McCall, *New Mexico in 1850: A Military View*, Norman, Okla.: University of Oklahoma Press, 1968.

William T. Jackson, *Wagon Roads West,* New Haven: Yale, 1965

On Top Again

AT THE END of the summer session, 1950, I was
suffering from an excess of analytical geometry
induced by Professor Gladman's Math 603, and felt a
great need to purify my soul in high places. My friend,
Danny Vickers, and I worked in the Texas Western
College Library when not in class, and had explored
all the possible routes of ascent and descent offered by
the empty dumbwaiter shaft back in the stacks, as well
as the grand traverse just below the roof-line. But we
hankered after wilder challenges, and in that last week
of classes and examinations, we decided to go north to
the Organs and climb that great and imposing tooth
of granite which was later to be called The Wedge. In
those days it had no name, and we were young.

We had become familiar with the peak over many
hiking and climbing excursions up Fillmore Canyon,
Dripping Springs Canyon, and to the old Modoc mine
in search of galina specimens. Most of our trips ended
with a few hours of bouldering on the 40-foot chunks
shed over the thousands of millennia by the south face,
which loomed over us, buff-golden and horribly vertical, for more than a thousand feet. Our view of the

southeast ridge showed it beginning with what looked like a 50-foot overhang, and the only line of approach that seemed within our abilities was by the west. There we must find a way through the complexly broken shoulder to a deep gully which ran to within 130 feet of the top. We saw no route on those last 300 feet, but they were far away, and we felt if we could get to the notch, we would find a way to the summit.

David Burwell had discovered rock climbing at the same time we had, four years before, and we had climbed together steadily since then every peak and the whole ridge of the Franklins, Hueco Tanks, Mc-Kittrick and Slaughter Canyons in the Guadalupes, and assorted buildings and retaining walls around El Paso. He, too, was eager for glory and adventure before his senior year at Cathedral High School began. We decided to make a weekend of it, and on a Friday afternoon gathered our gear and set out in Danny s jeep. I smile when I remember our "gear." We had no climbing rope, and though we had read about such arcana as pitons and caribiners, we had never seen any. We had rough boots well broken-in by mountain miles, each an odd pack—mine was a surplus Army Bergen with a steel frame—a sleeping bag, web belt and Army canteen, Levis and work shirts. Some canned fruit, beans, dried apricots, hard candy, and that's about it. Simple folk with simple needs, though inflamed by a wild desire.

That night we camped at Las Cuevas, and after entertaining ourselves on those delightful faces till dusk, we watched the last of the sunlight play on the face of The Wedge. It was so high and inviolable above us that it was hard to imagine that we could be on top by noon next day.

.

Thirty-four years later a road has been cut nearly to the Modoc, though it takes a stout four-wheeler to make it all the way. Dick Ingraham and I walk slowly up the last mile of the road. He is patient with me as I am humping a 50-pound pack, loaded with water for three days, and have lived for the past 14 years in the Black Swamp, elevation 600 feet. When we pass the Modoc the memory comes sharp of its dark stopes and tunnels, and its one deep shaft. I am no longer curious about its secrets, for we went everywhere in it except up or down that shaft. In the old days, after bouldering, we would come here to relax in the cool dark to plan our supper and tomorrow's conquests.

This morning is a curious amalgam of time present with time past, and I am alternately, simultaneously on the same path, separated by near three and a half decades. David and Danny and I had left our path at Las Cuevas, pocketed some candy and an orange, filled our canteens and struck out at dawn. We were old hands at minimalism, and moved with practiced speed. Today I feel the heavy bear inside me, and the weight of more water than I had ever seen in the Organs before. Years may have increased my ambition, but not the means to achieve it.

From the Modoc, the trail, such as it is, runs east over the swell of a hill, then up a steep slope to the saddle behind the prominence marked 7464 on my USGS map. The brush has been mild so far by Organ standards, and the only tedious obstacle I have had to fight has been the skree which makes each step an uncertainty. I cannot be agile with such a load, so must be careful. I plan to camp at the saddle, and will leave most of my burden there, The thought of shedding my pack makes the last 50 steep yards nearly pleasant. Dick and I take a short rest as I get down to basics of canteen, dried apricots, a candy bar, and my windbreaker. The saddle is classically formed, grassy, and there is an old piñon downed beside a spot level enough for sleep. To the west, Las Cruces seems to lie just beneath the distant Florida mountains.

The next quarter mile I remember well from 34 years before. It is a jumble of broken cliffs, impossible thickets of cactus and brush, and offers ten wrong choices to make for every right. Organ brush is in a class with the meanest in the world. I have struggled with aggressive alder thickets in Alaska, and salal on the Olympic Peninsula, and I have bucked my way slowly and carefully through Southeast Asian and Indian jungles, and through mesquite in Sonora growing more thickly than mesquite is supposed to grow. But nothing quite beats Organ brush for the speed with which it can induce acute frustration and exhaustion. The only way through it, as Dick says in his incomparable *A Climbing Guide to the Organ Mountains*, is to "think like a deer." Now deer are smart enough not to want to go a good many places climbers want to go, so the advice only partly works. The first time up, Danny and David and I had studied this section for some long minutes, and then slipped into the brush, each choosing a slightly different route. We were all great leaders and unwilling followers, and our expeditions were less coordinated efforts than parallel ones. We liked it that way. David hated brush and would take to the rock at every opportunity, though this would often force him to dangerous passages. Danny was stoic and efficient, and plotted his route like a navigator. I rather liked brush, and found some joy in wriggling through it, and took each snag as an opportunity to notice small things. I like to think Organ brush taught me patience and sharpened my powers of observation. It still takes about an hour to manage the quarter-mile. And when you emerge into the spillway of the deep cleft that separates The Wedge from Lost Peak, your battle with brush is not over. The cleft is choked with brush. It is steep, and often the walls are no more than an arm's width apart.

Halfway up the cleft, a great stone has wedged itself, and poses a problem for the traveler. Today it is normal to move back under the cap-stone and climb a narrow chimney to an exit hole. I don't know why we didn't do that long age. Perhaps we didn't see the hole. Instead, we scaled the wall—a fairly delicate matter of friction and small holds. David, as usual, went farther and higher than Danny and I and perched for five minutes or so complaining and exalting of his fate as we watched nervously, before he made a deft leap to a nubbin of green stuff which he hoped might be rock. It was. From there to the notch was as quick then as it was now, and we stood a thousand feet above the saddle, hidden behind the jumble of rocks below. The last 250 feet remain. This time, both Dick and I knew exactly where to go. But back when the world was younger, and no one, as far as we knew, had ever stood where we did facing the problem of where to go from here, it was a matter for discussion and augury. The diretissima, right up the North Face, seemed a bit risky for solo climbers, as it is today. Now, when that route is taken, good ropework and the proper place-ment of chocks and runners are required for safety. We wisely decided against that route in 1950. But to take a bend sinister, angling up to the left, seemed reasonable, and we made a hundred or so feet over simple stacked boulders and segments of mountain top. There the route steepened seriously, and the line seemed to be up the east face, and to the right. At this point Dick and I roped up, and I fed him a belay as he climbed with the grace of a master up a pitch requiring friction, jam, and a sort of off-center layback. I remembered this pitch as I would remember the face of a mugger. It was here that we three gathered, studying the rock as some Holy Writ containing the message of salvation. It was hard, but not terribly hard. The problem was that without a rope, a fall would be undeniably fatal. We had no rope. But we had Danny, 180 pounds of football and mountain hardened muscle and steadiness. He propped himself against the cliff, and I grasped his shoulders, stepped on his bent calf, his hip, his shoulder, and, still searching for a hold above, on top of his crew-cut head. There was a hold, and a place to dangle a leg from, a makeshift rope for the others, and the rest was a high scramble to the top.

I swarmed up the hard spot this time, guaranteed a longer life by Dick's belay from above, and was quickly again on top of The Wedge. The tip of the peak was covered with Ladybugs—as it had been 34 years ago. I let the emotions of satisfaction and nostalgia have their due, and said the names of my first companions, and took in the stupendous view. I could see down the spine of the Organs to the Franklins and beyond to the Burros, south of Juarez. The Sacramentos loomed grey to the east, though the Guadalupes were obscured by the drift of El Paso's smog. Cerro Alto and the Huecos were clear. West, I could make out the edge of the Chiracahuas behind the serried Floridas, Cedars, Hatchitas, and the Animas. When I am on top, I have the eyes of an eagle. One reason I climb mountains is to make my bifocals irrelevant for awhile. To the north, the San Andres continued on through the infinity of the Jornada del Muerto, and there to the northwest was the complex of the Mimbres, the Black, and the

San Mateo, where I would soon be camped. It is only in those days in which love is rediscovered, or when a child is born, or by a single gesture reveals itself most precious and special, when some sudden insight dawns and life is momentously joyous, that I find comparison with those times on mountaintops.

Living these years in Ohio, bereft of mountains, I have taken up parachute jumping for the view and the sense of exposure. It is a pleasant way to spend three minutes, but it is too soon over. Running and cross-country skiing are wonderful exercises, but without mountains, not much more. I am a desert rat and a rock climber, not a woodsman, so the wonders of Michigan and Ontario appear to me most modest. I cannot see far enough in the woods. I confess I have thought of climbing the oaks on my place and stringing cables for traverses, or trying to grow rock. But these are the whimsies of an old man who now has to get down the mountain and return to Ohio.

With a rope, it's easy. I abseiled down the pitch it had taken me and David and Danny a cautious quarter hour to descend. And there the paths of past and present split. In 1950 we circled round to the south and under the great wall. The brush was so thick we could walk on it some feet above the ground, like treading water in a kelp bed, though I finally found crawling under it was easier. We moved farther apart in the descent than before, and straggled into the Modoc quite apart and beat as much from thirst as fatigue. It had been a long August day on one canteen. Dick and I took the cleft back and by five o'clock were at my camp. We offered some Wild Turkey to the heights, now booming in the late sunshine above us, and it was time for Dick to get on home. I would stay for another day and night to feed myself on the rushing solitude the Organs provide those who linger. One thing I should mention is the low cairn of rocks we found at the top in 1950, the rusted Prince Albert can inside, secured with some baling wire. There was a note in it that went this way:

> Top of the Organs, N.M., I have climbed mountains in Calif., Colo., Ariz., and Mex., but this is the toughest "little" mountain I have ever tackled. Arriving at this point May 17, 1934. Gratifies a 15 year wish to climb the Organs and I am well satisfied.
>
> Thinking there are few other dam fools like myself I am now going to bet a $5.00 fountain pen that anybody can win, if he will send to me by mail, within the next ten years this identical note here written by me.
>
> Steven H. Christensen, 1125 Shell Boulevard, Houston.
>
> P.S. I will also do my best to entertain you if you are ever in my city. S.H.C.

So we weren't the first, and six years late to collect the fountain pen. But Steve Christensen was more than a gentleman, and a few months later when he passed through, he took us to dinner at the Del Norte, and handed us each a check. Wherever he is now, I hope he has mountains to climb. And I echo W. Gorrell, Jr., and Don Button, who climbed the peak in 1954, thinking it was the highest unclimbed mountain in America, discovered our copy of Christensen's note, and wrote that "lacking some other name, we continued to call that rock the 'wedge,' but a better name might be 'Christensen Peak.'"